MW00774618

Two Centuries of Beautiful Dolls

by John Darcy Noble

Published by Hobby House Press, Inc.
Grantsville, Maryland 21536

Book design by Brenda L. Wiseman

Additional copies of this book may be purchased at $29.95 (plus postage and handling) from

Hobby House Press, Inc.

1 Corporate Drive

Grantsville, MD 21536

1-800-554-1447

www.hobbyhouse.com

or from your favorite bookstore or dealer.

©2000 John Darcy Noble

All rights reserved. No part of this book may be reproduced or utilized in any form or by any means, electronic or mechanical, including photocopying, recording, or by any information storage and retrieval system, without permission in writing from the publisher. Inquiries should be addressed to Hobby House Press, Inc., 1 Corporate Drive, Grantsville, MD 21536.

ISBN: 0-87588-527-6

Dedication

To the Memory of
Elizabeth De Burgo

It is not every man who can say that there was once a faerie Princess in his life.

Acknowledgements

In the front of most books on decorative arts, one finds a list of names, gracefully dedicated to "Those without whom this book could not have existed." I find that my own list is a lengthy one, since I have been passionately involved with my subject for over seventy years, during which time there have been many wonderful friends, to whom I owe a great deal, both for support and encouragement, but also for the sharing of precious, hard-to-acquire knowledge.

First and foremost of these is my beloved Vivien Greene, who blessed me long ago with her magical friendship. With the late Marguerite Fawdry, my dolls and I were priviledged to be founder-curators of the now world famous Pollock's Toy Museum in London. In those early days in England, there were few collectors of old playthings, but Laura Tresco, she of the sharp eyes and exquisite taste, was a friendly rival, while Irene Blair Hickman sped in and out of my life on her ancient bicycle. Both became dear friends who shared their passion for old dolls with me. And from this time dates my lifelong friendship with a young art student, David Walker, who was to become the illustrious world-renown stage designer. "Since my childhood I have always looked at things," says David, "but it was you who helped me to see them." David is now and avid doll and doll house collector.

When I came to America in 1960 I was sought out, to my amazement, by Dorothy Coleman. She and her daughters Ann and the late Jane introduced me to the late E.J. Carter, and we quickly became the jolliest of groups in spite of the miles between us. And it was the Colemans who led me, wide-eyed with amazement, into the far-flung world of doll collectors.

From amongst my special friends in this enchanted world, I must here say thank you to the list of well-wishers who so generously lent both their treasures and their expertise to enrich these pages. And this list, I am happy to say, is also a long one. So alphabetically, my most grateful thanks to: Norma Bessouet; Michael Canadas; Dorothy Dixon; Caroline Edleman; Fred and Stephanie Farago; Christiane Grafnitz; my longtime assistant and dear friend, Jane Hirschkowitz; Estelle Johnston; Peggy Lancaster; Winnie Langley; Dorothy McGonagle; that benign witch, Meriel Marlar; Margaret Molnar; Marygray O'Brown; Kit Robbins; Michael Stennet; François Theimer; Cara Varnell; Margaret Whitton; and of course, the amazing, mercurial Richard Wright.

A very special thank you, with much love, to my dear friend and editor, Carolyn Cook. If my book conveys to its readers the magic and enchantments of its subject matter, it is all Carolyn's doing. And there have been many delays during the birth pangs of this opus, and many thanks are due to the staff at Hobby House who have borne with them valiantly.

And final, fond thanks to my lifetime companion, Bishop Robert Clement who has so cheerfully put up with it all!

Mezzotint from a portrait of a child, circa 1750, artist unknown.

Table of Contents

Rare & Lovely

A revised edition of my beloved old book: "A Treasury of Beautiful Dolls"

This book, a personal "Treasury," was first published in 1971, nearly 30 years ago, when the climate of the doll world was very different. At that time, the concept of dolls as fine art scarcely existed, and collectors were concentrating almost exclusively on antique examples. My dear friends, the Colemans, who provided the foreword for that first book, had only just embarked on their extensive research, and most of the field was still poorly documented.

So much has happened since then, and for my "Treasury" to be republished now, with value for today's collectors, I feel that considerable revision is needed. The central parts of that book dealt with dolls from the later 19th and early 20th centuries, dolls which have since been extensively researched and written about. On the other hand, although a great many wonderful dolls from the 18th century - and even earlier - have come to light, about these we still know very little. Church figures, too, neglected in the 1960s, are now properly valued, and their influence on the development of children's dolls is freely acknowledged. Thus, one chapter from the old book can easily be developed into four.

Passionate as I have always been about old dolls and toys, they form only part of the wide spectrum of minor decorative arts that I have loved and collected since my childhood. Indeed, I have always considered myself a social historian, rather than a "doll expert." My fascination with the historical and philosophical implications of doll making, both past and present, was reflected in the original book. Indeed, this, I believe, is one of the reasons why, over the years, so many people have found it fascinating and exciting, and have urged me to republish.

In reframing these chapters, I have borne this consideration very much in mind, and I believe that this newly edited "Treasury" provides a personal view of the magical world of dolls that is as fresh and interesting as it was in the original book. And it takes up where that now much outdated volume left off.

I think I should stress here that this book is not - and was never intended to be - a history of doll making. It is rather a scrapbook, a series of dolls pulled out of the passing parade as examples of the astonishing variety of these beloved toys, as well as of their importance, both as historical documents and as valid works of art.

For the dolls that grace these pages are, all of them, to my mind, both rare and lovely.

John Darcy Noble

Foreword

A slight frame and twinkling eyes do not predict the imaginative dynamo that is John Darcy Noble. Over the past five decades the Coleman's paths have crossed with this totally engaging person on both sides of the Atlantic, and memorably, on many occasions have co-existed.

Dorothy and Jane saw his first exhibition in London in the 1950s when the Colemans were first beginning to collect antique dolls. The small gray-covered catalogue was probably the first publication on antique dolls to enter the Coleman library.

Ann met the man in 1964 immediately after stepping off a trans-Atlantic liner. At this point he was already the internationally respected Curator of Toys at the Museum of the City of New York. Here he would, as never before, bring both old and new toys to life in magical exhibitions, imaginative publications, and as he researched and collected for the museum.

Jane would join his museum team: she brought what he called "eagle eyes" and information, he supplied intelligence and creativity. After all, his nimble mind is matched by nimble fingers.

Ann would chauffeur him-and frequently voiceless dolls-to meetings and photo shoots for his publications, including the forerunner of this volume. Wherever they went it was an adventuresome exploration.

With Dorothy, American home-style hospitality could be found and with the Coleman's collection at hand there was a catalyst for creative conversation. Shared friends, shared memories and a shared love of dolls have all made John a special feature in the lives of the Colemans.

But beyond that, John Darcy Noble has been a beacon. He carries a light, the light that understanding the role of dolls need not fade as childhood does. Rather, as John shows us, with the right mind and sense of delight, dolls can continue to captivate and inform.

Follow his byways and you will be treated to visual, cultural and material delights. The Colemans have followed this Pied Piper of dolls for nearly half century and have never been disappointed; neither will you.

Dorothy and Elizabeth Ann Coleman

Boston 1999

Introduction

Grottoes and garden follies, snuffboxes and shell-work, Valentines and Victoriana, puppets, post-cards, tramp-art and the Toy Theatre: from my earliest years such minor decorative arts have held for me an intense fascination, being as they are the offshoots, the outer edges of aesthetic experience. The eccentric, the morbid, the frivolous and the trivial, the excessively familiar and therefore overlooked – they compel my attention and enthral my mind.

Of all such delights, the fascination with old dolls is the quintessential one. It has distracted me for years, leading me down remote and dream-like paths to the disparate places where old dolls can be found, and introducing me to rare, magical people. Of my many diffuse interests amongst the arts and minor arts, none has been so rewarding as this obsession with dolls, and especially with the dolls that I, personally, consider beautiful.

I believe that, as long as there have been children – and especially little girls – and as long as play has been a natural function of human beings, there has always been some kind of doll for those children to play with. But the further back in time that we reach, the deeper the mists in which those children and their toys are lost, although there are always tantalising hints – a painting of a little girl holding an unmistakable doll, for instance, or a mysterious, doll-like object found after being hidden for centuries in an ancient cupboard.

And the further back we look, the less clear the distinction between the child and the adult, especially amongst the upper echelons, the aristocratic children who were the only ones, in those remote days, for whom dolls were especially made. When a girl could be engaged at the age of ten and married and the mistress of a great house by the age of 14, was she a child or a grown-up as she put her splendid wooden doll to sleep in its canopy bed?

Here is a rich field for romantic conjecture. I have chosen to begin this exploration in Europe, and in the early 18th Century when very recognisable dolls were suddenly plentiful, for in my old age, I am drawn more and more towards the earlier and more mysterious examples. There must regretfully be limitations, even to the most sumptuous of books, and here I have covered one and a half centuries, ending with the lovely early French porcelain-headed ladies of the early 1850s, as costly and extravagant as anything that proceeded them.

This book is not intended as a history, nor as any kind of guide or textbook – such things exist already, and are written far more competently than I ever could. Rather, it is an attempt to demonstrate in some measure the kaleidoscopic and seemingly infinite variety of dolls made in the past for both children and, in perhaps surprisingly large numbers, for grown-ups. And it will demonstrate, I hope conclusively, that doll making is not such a minor matter, after all. Indeed, I believe it can often take a place legitimately amongst the fine arts, alongside drawing, painting and sculpture.

This is my personal belief, and this book is a personal selection of dolls carefully chosen from amongst many lovely examples available. As my title suggests, these dolls are rare, and some of them are perhaps unique. Many have never been seen in print before. And the author has had the rare pleasure of being guided by his own preferences rather than by other considerations.

John Darcy Noble

From "Galeriedes Modes," published in Paris, 1780.

Virgins & Angels

The first thing one asks when confronted with the magical, vivid, pulsating presence of an ancient doll is, "From whence came all the various skills needed to produce such an entity? What are the antecedents for this doll – where did it come from?" There is no one complete answer, but in the case of the early European dolls, we can find at least one very direct source in the Roman Catholic churches. All of them at the time we are considering were crowded with shrines to the Virgin Mary, as well as to many saints and angels, and all contained statues.

The statues in such shrines were of various ages, but in many instances, the contemporary ones were made exactly like the dolls with which we are perhaps more familiar. They were carved from wood, and had articulated limbs, glass eyes and real hair wigs – and often, in the case of female saints, were dressed in the height of contemporary fashion. Here, surely, was one very rich source for doll makers. Indeed, I suspect that the early doll makers were the very same artisans who made the church figures, and who would readily accept commissions to make dolls for the privileged children of aristocratic parents.

La Dolorosa, fragment, Italian, circa 1730

This beautiful fragment represents the sorrowful Virgin. How can we be sure of this? At the base of the carving, just below the waist, there are six square slots cut, and these would have accommodated the struts of a cage-like base to the figure. Traditionally, it would have been considered highly improper and irreverent to represent the lower limbs of the Virgin, and so, although all other female effigies are found with legs, stockings, shoes and sometimes fascinating, archaic sandals, the Virgin is always recognisable by her distinctive cage base.

Here too, we can find below the shoulders the round openings for the missing, articulated arms, and the bald skull has a painted black cap where a wig or perhaps a wimple would have been placed.

The carving, together with the painting, is bold and strong, and the impression of intense grief is overwhelming. A touching and most moving detail is the presence of tears, five of them, on the Virgin's cheeks. They are carved from crystal, and have been set with patience and skill deep into the wooden cheeks.

Crude enough, perhaps, to be considered Folk Art, this fragment is nevertheless, by any standards, a masterpiece.

St. Elizabeth, Italian, 17th century (her dress circa 1750)

This large saint was given to me by a collector friend, a rich lady who bought dolls the way other women buy groceries. "This was with a batch of French bébés I just got," she said. "It's terribly battered, but you might be able to use the body, and the face isn't bad. Otherwise, just throw it away!" I thanked her kindly, and then carried the figure home most carefully, for already I had no intentions of throwing it away!

It was indeed sadly battered. The tall body was a wire armature, padded with straw and wrapped with strips of unbleached linen. The papier-mâché head hung precariously, for the backs of the neck and shoulders were broken away, and every finger had been broken, leaving gruesome stumps for hands. Strands of filthy hair clung to the head, reminding me of an Egyptian mummy.

There were the remains of a silken dress, the front of which was hanging in tatters, together with the shreds of a silken veil. Centuries of smoke from a candle rack, together with the effects of seasonal damp and cold, had eroded the fabric. The front of the dress had almost rotted away.

This was nevertheless a figure of exceptional quality. It represented a woman saint dressed in the height of fashion for the mid-18th century. The ivory-coloured silk was hand-painted with a repeat pattern of formalised flowers. These dresses would be made up in plain silk and then sent to China to be painted – a costly and time-consuming process. Treasured, such a dress was often bequeathed to the Church, where nuns would convert the rare fabric into vestments. Leftover fragments were hoarded and used for such figures as this one.

Expert opinion suggested that the figure was decidedly from the mid-17th century, while the dress was from the 1750s, at least 100 years later.

Restoration of the fabric was undertaken by Margaret Molnar, a graduate of the prestigious school of conservation near Bern, Switzerland. It was no light task, and took over four years. The blue silk veil was then stabilised and the human hair wig was carefully washed and provided with a new linen cap. The faux pearls at the neck and wrist proved to be 18th century wax ones, which were cleaned and restrung on linen thread.

Meanwhile, the damage to the head and hands was made good by another expert, Norma Bessouet. A painter from Argentina, she had been taught the almost forgotten traditional papier-mâché craft by an old church-image maker in Barcelona. Norma's replacements are undetectable.

The last stage of this long restoration was achieved by Cara Varnell, a conservationist at the Los Angeles County Museum of Art, who was introduced to me by a mutual acquaintance, Edward Maeder, who at that time was Curator of Costume and Textiles. These two good friends, working together, strengthened and secured the crumbling linen body so that the dress fell easily into place, with the hemlines, the sleeves and the folds all taking up their original positions. The figure now has authority and assurance.

A long and costly process, but infinitely worthwhile. I acquired three good new friends, and the figure regained her unique beauty. She needed a name, and I chose to call her Saint Elizabeth the canonised Queen of Hungary.

Virgin & Child, fragment, Neapolitan, circa 1790

Here again, there is evidence of the telltale cage skirt, which in this case has been crudely sawn away for some unimaginable reason. Some day it, too, shall be replaced, and this lovely group dressed as befits its quality. For here is the craft of the church-figure maker to be seen at its zenith, generations of skill culminating in perfection.

The carving here is assured and masterly, and yet has a soft, even tender quality which bespeaks a master craftsman. This is a very sweet group, but by no means sentimental - the Virgin is thoughtful, but very aware, while the child is alert, brimming with vitality.

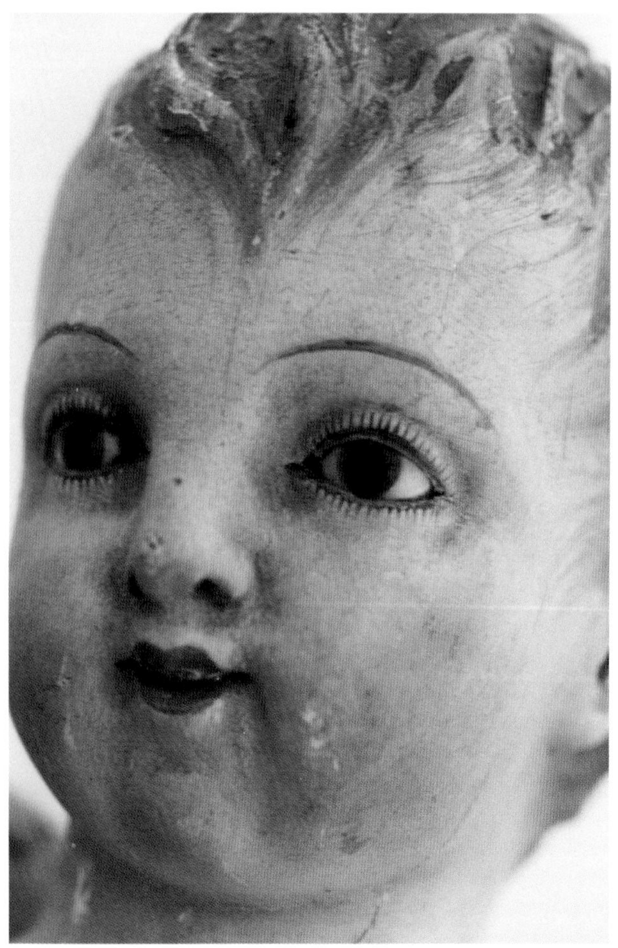

Neapolitan Virgin and child, circa 1790, described on page 16.

St. Dorothy, the Mysterious Lady & Child, circa 1750

It was through Richard Wright that I heard about this fascinating pair, and it is by the gracious permission of their present owner, Caroline Edleman, that we are able to contemplate them here.

They are certainly 18th century, and from the style of their carving, I should imagine a Latin origin, Spanish or Italian. They were found wearing brocade dresses, like other church figures, and I believe that this is what they were intended for. But they are quite unlike any others I have seen. They find a place here, in this book, because both the style of the carving and the system of articulation, with pegged joints, can be found on many children's dolls of this period. In fact, their previous owner wondered if they were not in fact originally dolls, despite the brocaded dresses and the child's crown.

This reinforces my theory that those early dolls, from Catholic countries at least, were often the work of craftsmen whose traditional skills for making church figures had been handed down for centuries.

The first thing to notice is that the lady has legs, so this pair cannot have been made as the Virgin and child. But it is quite obvious that they were carved by the same hands, and were intended as a pair. Secondly, the lady is carved with a young figure, with a narrow waist and breasts, not the usual, discreet mono-bosom.

I was much struck by the great beauty and delicacy of the carving and the distinct personalities with which both figures are imbued. The lady in particular has a haunting face, with a curious, twisted smile. These are not standard, run-of-the-mill figures. I imagine a special commission, perhaps to honour the patron saint of the church for which they were intended.

But which saint? I delved into my research books to find a woman saint who would be depicted with a child, and the first one to surface was St. Dorothy. Her story is fascinating and romantic, and curiously enough, fits perfectly the attitudes and expressions of these two figures.

Dorothy was a Roman maiden who converted to Christianity. She was arrested and persecuted for her new faith and threatened with death. Her lover, a Roman Centurion, pleaded with her. "All you have to do is renounce this new religion," he said, "And I swear I will make you happy – I will make your life a bed of roses." But Dorothy smiled at him. "I shall have roses enough in Heaven," she said "And they will never fade, like earthly roses."

So she was executed, and her grief-stricken lover attended the Mass for her soul, performed very secretly in the catacombs. And when the priest raised the chalice at the climax of the ceremony, a shower of roses fell from the air and covered the altar! And her lover was converted.

St. Dorothy is depicted, in church paintings and statuary, as a young girl with flowing hair, and she is always leading – or carrying – the infant Jesus. He is sometimes a toddler and sometimes a babe in arms, but always he holds a basket full of roses. Sometimes he hands one to her.

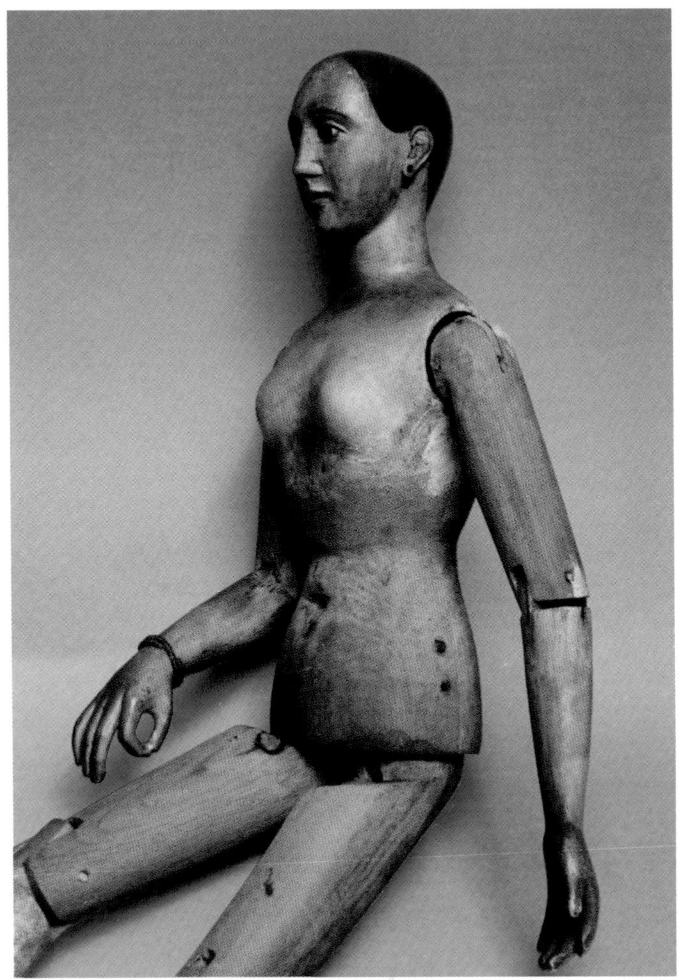

Turning to Caroline's figures, I saw that each right hand has its thumb and first finger held together, a position perfect for holding a rose, while the child's left hand is turned downwards, a gesture I have never seen before in any church figure, and it could easily be holding a basket. The child is in a sitting position, and the girl's left arm is jointed so that it will only move straight up and down, the hand held out flat to support the child – or a basket?

I offer this explanation not as a fact, but as a possibility. It would explain this fascinating pair, and would also account for the curious, slightly twisted smile that is carved onto the girl's mouth. For of all the saints, St. Dorothy certainly did have the last laugh!

There is no way of knowing, or of confirming my theory. But Caroline is left with a wonderful work of art, and I am happy in the assurance that, as long as she owns them, these lovely figures will stay together.

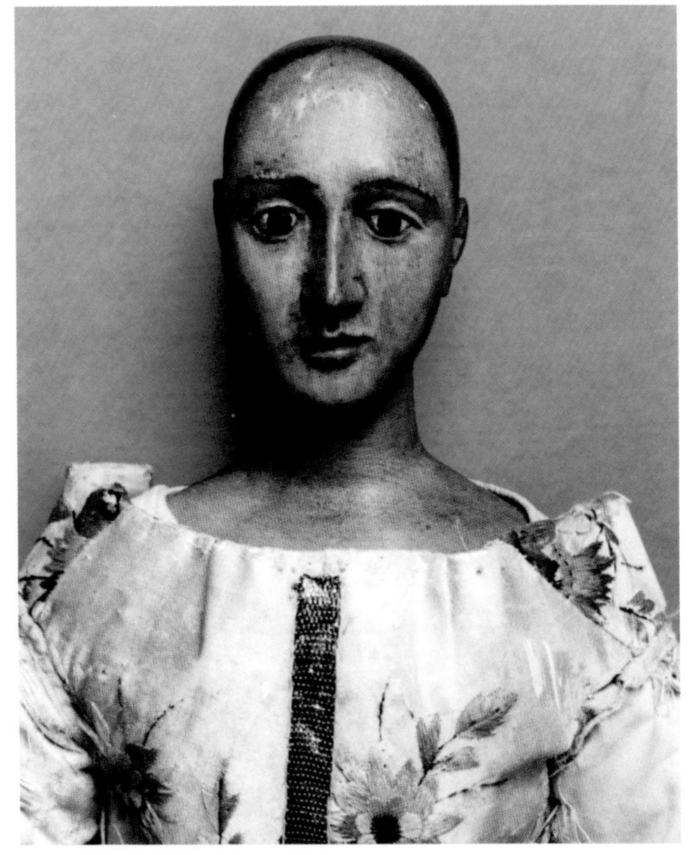

Christ child, German, mid-18th century

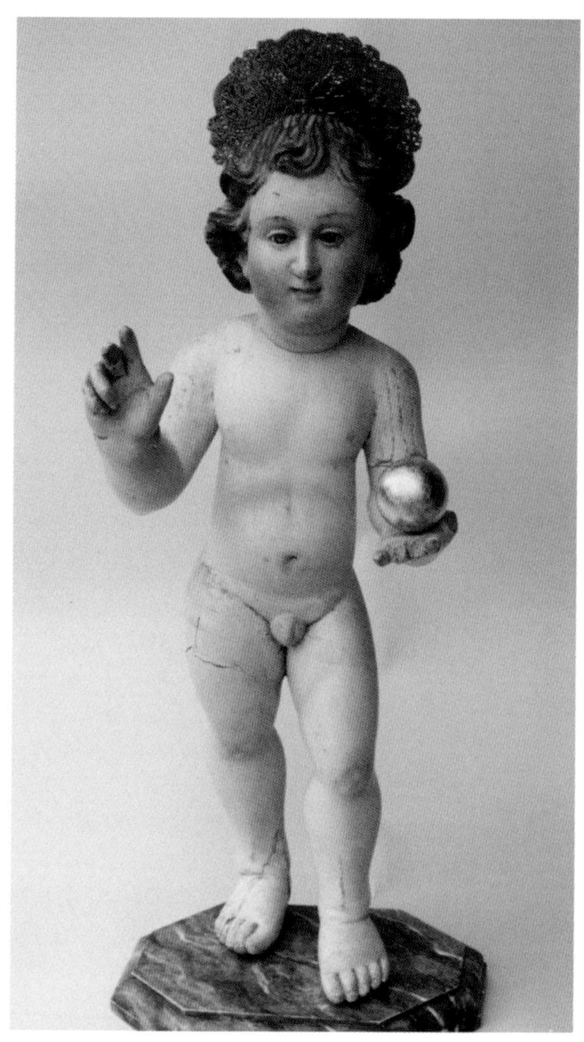

This little fellow was found some 30 years ago in Germany by another collector, but had I not known this, I would have guessed its origin. The German church figures often have a subtle, elusive quality, which is nevertheless instantly recognisable – a quiet reserve, withdrawn and contemplative, unlike the emotional, heart-on-the-sleeve figures from Italy and Spain.

He was found in an antique shop in Munich. The late 1960s had seen drastic reforms within the Catholic Church and for a few years thereafter, wonderful treasures like this statue could be found by anyone with a discerning eye – and a taste for such things.

This child is of carved wood: I suspect lime, apple or one of the other softer woods, which lend themselves to delicate carving. The work here, although slightly but engagingly naïve, is most careful and loving, and the artist has achieved a curious tenderness, which is very appealing. The hair is carved, but the eyes are inset glass with reverse painting, i.e., the details of pupil, iris and whites are rendered inside the glass sphere, a detail which has preserved these, and the eyes of many other statues of this period, from detriment.

This is clearly the work of a master craftsman. He was not a major artist, but his obvious devotion and love of his work has indeed produced an enchanting work of art.

Baroque Angel, circa 1730

German? Carved wooden figure, with heavy features, carved wooden wings. The velvet costume, based on the Roman soldier, is sumptuously ornamented with gold bullion braiding and fringe. It features a version of the *tonnelet. Collection of Estelle Johnston.*

Virgin with Tinsel Wreath, German, mid-18th century

I contemplate this tiny figure (for she is barely eight inches high) with great satisfaction, for in her case my own theory, held by many to be far-fetched, turns out to have been correct.

I found her in a grubby junk shop in one of the poorest parts of New York sometime in the 1970s. She looked so lost and woebegone, standing alone amongst a conglomeration of mismatched dishes and pots and pans. She was covered with dust, and she cost almost nothing.

After very careful vacuuming, she began to look much better. The superficial dust came away easily from the crumpled brocades, which underneath were in fact quite clean. The clothes could not be removed: they are sewn and in places glued into position. But careful steaming straightened them, and as so often happens with old garments, they fell back into their original positions. The tinsel wreath with its tiny coral beads I rinsed quickly in hot water. It dried almost instantly, and to my great relief looked almost new.

The head and body are papier-mâché, with moulded and painted hair. There are no lower limbs, the trunk evolving into a very simply modelled floor-length papier-mâché petticoat, the brocade robe, and a brocade mantel that falls from the shoulders. There are no arms, the hands being sewn into the sleeves above the wide cuffs of the old lace – which transpires to be hand-made.

"But it isn't anything very special," said collector friends when I showed them. "It's just the top half of an early papier-mâché doll, tricked up to look like a Virgin. And very home-made, too!" But is it? I've lived with this pretty little thing for some 20 years now, and grow fonder of it all the time. And the longer it is with me, the more sure I am of its integrity.

I believe this is one sure way of telling a fake. However clever it may be, it can have no true identity, no soul. And sooner or later, the more familiar one becomes with it, this lack of reality will become more and more obvious. But not so with my little Virgin – in my eyes, at any rate.

She has recently been loaned to the prestigious exhibition, "Dolls, Mirrors of Humanity" at the Mingei International Museum in Balboa Park, San Diego. Amongst many illustrious visitors, we were honoured to receive Christiane Grafnitz, one of the leading researchers in this area today. Christiane had very complimentary things to say about the old dolls in the exhibit – and she was delighted with the little Virgin.

"I've always loved her, too, although I have never been sure of her age," I said cautiously.

But Christiane nodded firmly. "She is 18th century, of course. I have seen them sometimes in Germany – but not often, for they are very rare."

"But she does look very much like an early 19th century doll...," I said.

"But of course she does," beamed Christiane. "After all, she is their ancestor!"

Yes, very satisfactory.

Italian Wax Christ Child, 18th century

I suspect that this wax Christ child is of either Neapolitan or Venetian origin. He is only seven inches high, so was most certainly intended for a private shrine. His elaborate costume, rich with bullion braiding, is for travelling, with a hooded cloak. This perhaps represents the Christ child as a pilgrim. *Collection of Dorothy McGonagle.*

Swaddled Christ Child, Late 18th century

This beautiful toy has come down to me in its original box, and my pleasure in it is enhanced by the signature of a previous owner, written carefully in pencil on the bottom of the box: "Mrs. De Witt Clinton Cohen." This lady was the wife of an important figure in New York's political history, in the early years of the 20th century, and she was also a pioneer doll collector, with both money and taste enough to acquire the best.

These swaddled babies are quite rare, but enough examples survive to prove that they were once standard toys, but from what source and for what purpose we do not exactly know. I can only offer my own theory.

From quite early days, in Catholic countries – Italy, France, Spain and even in Holland, Christmas was a sacred day. Dancing and merriment took place both before and after; firstly at the feast of St. Nicholas, the children's saint, on the sixth of December, and again on New Year's Eve. From St. Nicholas came many of today's traditions transferred to Christmas, including the visit of Santa Claus – the very saint himself.

Children left their shoes or wooden clogs by the chimney, just as some children still leave their stockings, to find in the morning a swaddled Christ child doll for a good girl, or a more active Christ child figure for a good boy, together with their shoes stuffed with candy and sugar plums. For bad children there was only a shoe full of coal and a hazel switch!

This, I believe, was the purpose of the figure here, with its waxen head, its beautiful embroidered and lace-trimmed swaddlings, and its halo of glittering tinsel. Such a figure was expensive and was treasured in its box to be looked at sometimes but never played with. Which is why some of them have come down to us in such perfect condition.

At least, this is my pet theory!

Strong Museum's Early 18th Century Wooden Doll

This urban lady in genteel attire, accession number 79.451, has finely sculpted features. Her gown is made of pink-bronze damask and it covers a billowing quilted petticoat. Her hat is made of the same damask material as her dress, and her elbow-length kid gloves are the perfect accessory to complete this fashionable early 18th century ensemble. *Collection of the Margaret Woodbury Strong Museum.*

Georgian Splendour

In this chapter, a few examples of 18th century dolls are examined. They have been included here chiefly to acknowledge the sharp line drawn across history by the Industrial Revolution. They help to demonstrate simply, both the differences in dolls before and after the emergence of the German toy-making industry at the end of the 18th century and the rapidly changing attitudes towards children that took place at the same time.

Although made for the offspring of the well-to-do, the common doll of the 18th century – a wooden one – was a remarkably crude affair, considering that its surviving examples are found chiefly in aristocratic houses. The bulk of such dolls, as far as we know, came from England, but recent research has traced manufacturers in several European countries, including Austria, Switzerland, France, Spain and Holland. Many of these dolls can be dated to the earlier decades of the 18th century.

These wooden "babies," as they were known in English-speaking countries, were not factory products. They were made by journeymen, working either in their own homes or, if itinerant, by the roadside. Often the dolls were a sideline to the manufacture of more mundane artifacts. A turner, when the demand for his furniture was slack, would take refuge in doll making, carving these toys with primitive skills born of long practice, or perhaps handed down through generations.

These "babies" would be dressed in the scraps and trimmings from the upsilks and sold either to haberdashery shops or to the ubiquitous bagmen, who travelled about the towns and countrysides with their carts, just as the pedestrian peddlers would do – hence the name given to the less pretentious of the 18th century woodens, "Bagmen's Babies."

Dolls such as these were still being made as late as the 1820s, although by this time the competition from mass-produced dolls was almost overwhelming. And slowly, as the wooden babies changed, they deteriorated in quality. The earlier dolls are always the finer ones. Into the roughly turned, basic form, their features were carved with a subtle awareness of personality and with remarkable vitality. One is very aware of the pride of a craftsman in an excellent product. As the century progressed, the carving gradually became slicker and more competent, and the heads more globular. Features became bunched and sharply linear, stylised from a set of three-dimensional planes into more or less mechanical graphs.

Apart from the quality of the work, these wooden babies are difficult to date since there are no patents, catalogues, or other dated documents. And a healthy, active craftsman could have produced his own version of a doll over a period of some 40 years, with few variations in his own particular style.

Thus, if he were also itinerant, his distinctive doll could have been scattered over the countryside in the space of nearly half a century, and might be found wearing the clothing style of 1730 or 1770, both equally original. How is one to date such dolls?

Bodmer 18th Century Wooden Doll

The most enviable of 18th century woodens, at least to my eyes, is this charmer, once part of the legendary Bodmer collection. Of European origin, the carving here is surely by a master, and the head is vibrantly lifelike – indeed, it has so much personality that one feels it must have been taken from life. The body, too, is most sensitively realized, with the curious bend at the waist, representing the posture imposed by a fashionable corset.

The clothing is all original and early, and the printed cotton (or linen?) apron is most interesting, for this is from copper plates, a technique invented in Dublin, Ireland, in the 1740s, and adopted shortly thereafter by a manufacturer in France. *Collection of Estelle Johnston.*

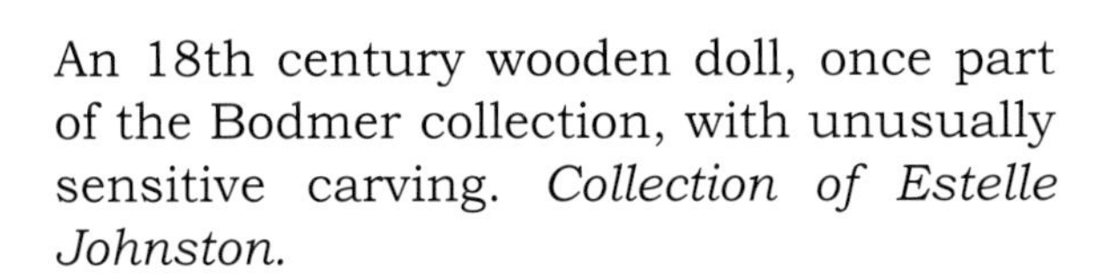

An 18th century wooden doll, once part of the Bodmer collection, with unusually sensitive carving. *Collection of Estelle Johnston.*

English Wooden Memorial Doll

Kept as a precious memorial to the beloved child who had owned her and who died so young, this lovely English doll from the 1730s was not framed in a shadowbox and hung in the parlour as was the custom of the time, but was stored away carefully in a capacious box, to be opened perhaps only on her birthday. Thus this doll has survived to us immaculate, miraculously untouched by time. *Collection of Dorothy Dixon.*

European Wooden Memorial Doll

An old friend and favorite of mine, this lovely early wooden doll has spent most of her life protected within her original glass case, no doubt as a memorial to a deceased child. She can date no later than 1735, I think, and from the subtle and sensitive carving of her features, I believe her to be of European rather than English origin. Costume is original, never disturbed in over 250 years. *Collection of Richard Wright.*

Peggy Lancaster's Wonderful Wooden Doll "Lady Pullen," A Rare and Early Delight

Of all the dolls made for children during the past four centuries – and there are many of them – none are more vibrant, more vivid, or more mysterious than those wooden wonders from the 17th and 18th centuries. At least, so it seems to this author, who has been delighting in them ever since he saw his first examples behind glass in the museums of London all of 70 years ago.

At that time, doll collecting as a hobby simply did not exist in England, and even in America it was in its infancy, confined to a few remarkably visionary women scattered across this vast continent, who were largely dismissed as "little old ladies in tennis shoes."

Even the serious collectors – those passionate pioneers like the Henry Francis DuPont brothers or Electra Havemeyer Webb in Vermont, all assiduously discovering and preserving America's heritage of decorative arts – even these erudites treated old toys as trivialities, picked up in passing to be used as "buttonholes" when the time came to present their collections to the public view.

For me, a little boy growing up in a Victorian backwater of London and slowly amassing my own humble collection of decorative arts with equal passion and single-mindedness, dolls and dolls' houses, as well as other toys from the past, exerted a powerful magic, but none more so than those rare early wooden ladies who gazed back at me from their glass cases in the V. and A. and in the London Museum; in Horniman's Museum, not far away in a neighbouring suburb; in the Rothschild house museum in Gunnersbury Park, and in other small, local, historical museums which it was my great pleasure to discover and to explore.

As I have said, doll collecting was still in its infancy, and I never saw these enigmatic dolls anywhere else. They never appeared in antique shops, as did occasionally the choicer specimens of French bisques and German chinas. Looking back, the reason is not hard to find. Those wooden dolls were still sleeping serenely, undiscovered, in the attics of stately homes all over England and New England. For it was clear, even in those early days, that these were aristocratic toys, owned only by the children of wealthy families.

I shall never forget the thrill of excitement when, in the mid-1950s, I was invited to help curate an exhibition of old toys, to be called "Children's Paradise," sponsored by the Royal Society for the Blind. It was to be housed over the Christmas season in a prestigious gallery in Park Lane. The Society could boast the support of several royal duchesses, so the toys were gathered up from very stately attics indeed.

Most of these aristocratic treasures were lent by collaterals of their original little owners, and amongst them were several glorious early wooden dolls, the first ones that I had ever had the privilege of handling and examining closely. It was then that it began to dawn on me that these alluring darlings were not so rare as I had imagined. And sure enough, as the decades passed and the collecting hobby flourished and became more and more organised, more and more of these wooden wonders appeared on the market. It was not long before the "Clapham" hoard appeared in a London auction house, with its attendant publicity, and I realised that there were dolls surviving from the 17th century as well as from the 18th.

Today, this is all old news. These wonderful dolls have taken their rightful places, both in our collections and in our hearts, as the *crème-de-la-crème* of the doll world, with their vibrancy and vitality and their elusive, haunting charm. Mostly, they have come down to us undisturbed, by virtue of their sheer monetary value. They usually escape the dire fate of so many later dolls, of being redressed, rewigged and even repainted out of all recognition. So they are most valuable social documents, offering us insights into the modes and manners of the past, more vividly and directly than any other surviving artifacts.

I came to America in 1960, and before long I had made many friends in the doll world and had the pleasure of seeing and examining many splendid collections. And it was in the early 1960s that I was given photographs of an especially beautiful early wooden – photographs which I treasure to this day, for it was a doll to whom I instantly lost my heart. It sat serenely under a glass "shade" in its owner's drawing room, and it was unlike any other 18th century example that I had ever seen. It belonged to a friendly collector, Marjorie Seibert, who alas lived far away, so I never saw the doll in person, not, that is, until the mid 1980s, and then only by a most fortuitous accident.

At that time, I was still collecting as avidly as anyone and I had many friends amongst dealers, but none so close as the legendary Richard Wright. Amongst my fondest memories of that remarkable decade are my numerous weekend visits, in all weathers, to his magical shop, buried in the depths of rural Pennsylvania.

Hidden away in the upper reaches of that amazing emporium, and out of bounds to most visitors, was the lair of Meriel Marlar, Richard's incredibly talented restorer, whom I have long considered to be a benign witch. For it seems that there are no miracles that Meriel cannot perform, and perform perfectly. Single-handedly, and in her chosen seclusion, she has raised the multiple and delicate arts of doll restoration to the levels of even the most advanced conservators in the world's most prestigious museums.

I am proud to be able to claim Meriel as a dear and close friend, and our friendship is of many years' standing. The forbidden studio was never forbidden to me, and some of the greatest pleasures of those visits were the enchanted hours in that remote attic studio, glimpsing

Meriel's work and gaining insights into not only her skills, but her peerless standards of restoration.

Here, one red-letter-day, laid carefully out on the worktable, was the late Marjorie Siebert's wooden doll. It had been acquired from Marjorie's effects by Peggy Lancaster, a contemporary collector of whose discerning tastes I was well aware. Besides its other excellencies, this doll can boast the identities of two of its earliest owners. It possesses an engraved card, the kind left in more leisurely days by a lady when visiting a house for the first time. It bears, in elegant script, the name "Lady Pullen," and on the reverse, in equally elegant copperplate, "This doll belonged to Mrs. J. Craven, about the year 1767." Assuming this to have been Mrs. Craven's own childhood toy, my conjecture of a very early date is thus confirmed.

The doll had suffered during the years it was in Marjorie's possession. Those early collectors, loving though they were, had only very sketchy ideas of conservation. The years under that glass shade, in both direct sunshine and bright electric light, as well as in wide range of shifting temperatures, had not been kind to the doll.

The very pure silk of the dress had survived fairly well, but the gesso on the face and neck had suffered. Due to the different shrinkage rates of the wood and the gesso, large pieces of the latter had come away and were either hanging perilously or had apparently disappeared. The astute Meriel, knowing the doll's history, had gained Peggy's permission to undress it, and sure enough, most of the missing gesso had fallen into the clothing and was safe.

When I saw this doll on that privileged afternoon, the restorations to the head were finished, but the clothing had not been replaced, so I had the rare opportunity to see the structure of the body, as well as a glimpse of the corset, usually hidden from sight. As can be imagined, I made careful notes. One fascinating detail is the carving of the doll's legs. Most of the English woodens of my acquaintance have lower limbs conceived with doll-like simplicity.

The carver of this doll, however, took as much care with her legs as he did with her face. Their delicate curves are carefully defined, and these elegant limbs terminate in tiny feet, enclosed in delicious, silken shoes. These have leather soles, each marked with pinpricks in the form of a floweret. Another enchanting detail is the beauty of the doll's gloves, of white kid and elbow length. These fit so perfectly that they must surely have been steamed into place – and of course, never removed in all of 260 years!

Peggy Lancaster is to be congratulated for having sensitivities that are only just now being shared by other collectors. For instance, there are the original metal loops, provided for earrings, and it would be sorely tempting to try to replace these ornaments. But Peggy resisted the temptation. Nor did she want new work to be added to the doll. So today, where gesso was missing, the slight chips to the forehead and about the eyes are still there, just as they are in many untouched old dolls. The

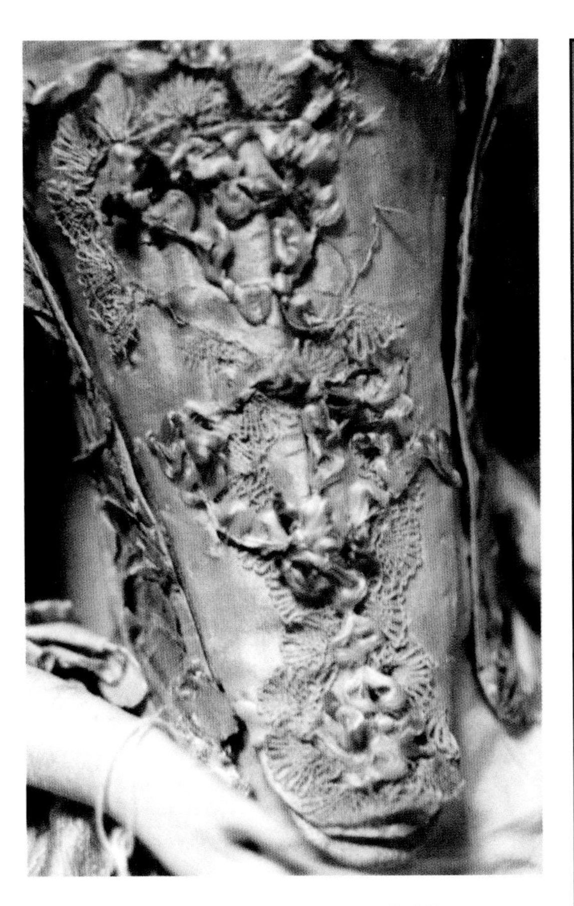

A detail of the Lancaster doll's stomacher.

This wooden doll, with its original human hair wig, has an engraved card which reads "Lady Pullen." The back of the card, in elegant copperplate, reads "This doll belonged to Mrs. J. Craven, about the year 1767." *Collection of Peggy Lancaster.*

gesso replaced by Meriel is, as might be expected, undetectable, so this doll appears to be untouched.

Thanks to Peggy Lancaster's kindness, we have photographs here of the redressed doll as it looks today. Needless to say, it is kept in museumlike conditions, stored in the dark with climate control and without the imposed strain of a doll stand. "When I want to look at it, or show it to others," says Peggy, "I can bring it out, for as long as there is interest. But it soon returns to its safe environment."

This is clearly not a run-of-the-mill doll. So many of the 18th century woodens in today's collections are English, but this, I am sure, is from the European continent, perhaps from Prussia or Austria. The carving of the face is subtle and telling, especially about the mouth, where a haunting, Mona Lisa-like smile is implied in the carving. The painting of the face is, too, quite remarkable, as light and delicate as that on Meissen figurines and with a treatment of eyebrows new to this author's experience.

The effect is far more sophisticated than that created by most other such woodens, and from the extremely fashionable dress with its wide panniers, I would guess its date to be between 1730 and 1740 – the Roccoco period. The wig, too, is most superior. Made of human hair, it retains its fashionable coiffure, small and round, typical of this period.

An interesting point here is that it is made of grey hair, representing powder. It is reported in one of the standard books on 18th century manners – a little research would discover the source – that it was fashionable at that time to wear one's own hair in the morning and grey powder in the afternoon; while for evening, white powder was "de rigour." The grey and white coiffures would almost certainly have been wigs.

The Lancaster doll is surely dressed for the afternoon, in her semiformal dress of striped silk. A fascinating detail is the wide train of a more heavily striped silk, with a second train, narrower and of the same silk as the rest of the dress. This is an unusual arrangement, never before seen by this observer, either in paintings or in fashion plates. She also wears an enchanting lace cap, with lappets tied under her chin. It is decorated with a posy of fly-fringe. As if this were not enough, the stomacher is held in place over the corset with its original, half-inch, handmade, two-part pins – these alone are as rare as hen's teeth. As this doll demonstrates, they were also an essential part of a lady's toilette, were expensive, and were the original need for a lady to have a constant supply of "pin money."

The reader must forgive my ecstasies. Faced with such a rare delight, the baldly objective approach, as my beloved Vivien Greene has observed, is well nigh impossible. It remains to thank Peggy Lancaster for her gracious permission to publish this story, and to praise Meriel Marlar, as much for her expertise and careful judgements as for her uncanny skills. I am not at all sure that she isn't a witch!

The Richest Doll in the World? Surely the Most Treasured and Pampered!

My friend Michael Stennet's English mid-18th century beauty gets given real, 18th century, rose-cut diamonds every year on her birthday! Michael is a famous English stage designer, and he himself created her dress and her wig. They are perfect enough to deceive experts!

Wooden Lay Figure

Although I have always looked for them on my travels, these old artists' mannequins are rare nowadays, but when they are encountered, it is always the same, an almost psychic experience. It is not just a wooden doll one meets, but also a personality – shadowy and elusive, but with a decided presence entirely its own. Too many other observers have felt the same way about such mannequins for my impressions to be dismissed as whimsical imaginings. For me, this is their magic, their special attraction.

Once made in many sizes, including even life-size, the rare 18th century lay figures are magical and haunting. But whatever their size, these wooden stand-ins were in constant use by portrait painters, enabling the clothes worn by their sitters to be translated onto the canvas without the imposed tedium of hours of posing.

Such lay figures were beautifully made, carved from soft wood (the Italian ones were traditionally made of lime-wood), which enables the features and the hands and feet to be finished in exquisite detail. And all were articulated, the more expensive ones with a waist and even spinal joints, so that the wooden figure could imitate almost any posture assumed by its human counterpart.

The gentleman in the red coat featured here is just such a lay figure, and I have known about him for a long time. In England, during the 1950s, a book called *Dolls and Puppets* was published by a passionate collector named Alice Early. It caused quite a stir, for at that time there were few English doll collectors and the only doll books we knew of were the American ones.

Mrs. Early was clearly a lady of financial substance, with taste and judgement. Many of the dolls with which she illustrated her book were unusual and exciting. I marvelled and coveted, but I was perhaps most intrigued with an unusual carved wooden figure.

It was a man, dressed in a priest's cassock. It had an unusual painted head. Thanks to my years at art school, I recognised this at once as an artist's lay figure, and an early one at that. Even in the gray photographs, his haunting presence was evident, and indeed, Mrs. Early commented in the text on the varying effects he had on his viewers. Some friends, she asserted, were afraid to be alone in the room with him!

I was young and impressionable, I suppose, but I have never forgotten that wooden figure with his strange, haunting face. My friend Vivien Greene has said in one of her books that if the cherished object is held in mind and loved steadfastly and faithfully, sooner or later it will be

This handsome lay-figure came from a 16th century Hall at Baddesley Clinton, complete with moat, where there is still a secret priests' hole, contrived during the grim days of Catholic persecution. *Collection of Dorothy Dixon.*

drawn to you – and so it has been with this figure—because only yesterday I held him!

He now belongs to my good friend, Dorothy Dixon. She has owned him for some time and in her possession he has slowly acquired other clothes, just as he might have done in an artist's studio, and his dashing red coat suits him very well.

He is tall and slender, and most beautifully carved, with long tapering hands. His head was long ago painted beautifully, but not professionally – that is to say, not with thin glazes of paint and varnish over a gesso foundation—but in one layer of oil paint, directly over the dark wood. This is obviously the work of his long-gone artist owner.

M. D'Allemagne's Mysterious Paper Angels

Some years ago, I was fortunate enough to acquire several old toys which had come from the legendary collection of Henri d'Allemagne, one of the first collectors of old toys, whose books about them, published in the early 1900s, are now themselves eagerly collected.

I was especially delighted to become the owner of a pair of large paper dolls, dressed in silks, brocades and tarnished bullion, which date from the mid-18th century. I had noticed such a doll many years before in a pamphlet concerning the paper toy collection of Wilbur Macey Stone. It was described as very rare, and I remembered it as very similar. Unfortunately, the pamphlet is lost or mislaid.

The d'Allemagne dolls are a foot high, their faces and limbs picked out in watercolour on thick, handmade rag paper. They are backed with thinner paper, and this has been mended and reinforced over the years. Crude, half-round dowels are sewn to the backs of the dolls with copper wire to provide the supports by which the dolls are mounted on wooden stands. None of this, I once felt, is original.

The dolls' costumes are highly stylised. A narrow corselet surmounts a wide skirt with panniers, and there are short, wide sleeves, all of this edged with silver gimp and embroidered with silver bullion. The faded colours were originally pinks and blues, and the dolls' heads wear painted crowns of roses. A gauze chemise provides full sleeves gathered just below the elbow, with ruffles matching those showing at the low neckline.

Each doll holds a painted heart in one hand, an enigmatic detail – but clues to the dolls' identities are to be found in the painted knots of ribbon below the knees, vestiges, I suspect, of breeches. Also, the dolls have stiff, formal wings, made from rows of shaded silk chenille.

These are angels, dressed as they so often were in elaborate crèche groups of their day, in the *tonnelet*, the stiff *pannier* worn over breeches by male dancers in the ballet. It was a stylised version of Roman armour. I remembered, too, that it was traditional for angels to wear crowns of roses.

Well and good, but I still knew far too little about my dolls. Who had made them, and for what purpose? And where? The ensuing research produced several fascinating discoveries.

First of all, a fragment of a similar doll is in the Maxine Waldron Collection at Winterthur. It is described as a dress made for a lost paper figure, a fashion model. The style and the materials are exactly the same as in the d'Allemagne angels. And not only is the one surviving hand drawn and even cut in just the same manner, but there are even vestiges of chenille wings. Clearly, here was a fourth angel.

Another was found shortly after in an engraving from the d'Allemagne book: *Histoire des Jouets*, (published in Paris in 1903). It shows a very similar doll, but lacking its crown, wings and heart – perhaps cut away by some agnostic parent? And in a bound volume of a French periodical of the early 1900s there were three more angels, with their wings and crowns intact, but all with broken or missing limbs. These too were from the collection of Henri d'Allemagne. We now had a record of eight very similar paper angels from the mid-18th century, amongst them two pairs. And six of them had belonged to Henri d'Allemagne.

A year later, I was lucky enough to acquire another such angel for myself. This one, too, came from the verbal tradition of a d'Allemagne provenance. It is smaller than my original pair – a mere ten inches tall – but very beautiful. It is in excellent condition, too, having been stored away (for who knows how long?) in an Italian wooden box, rich with carving and gold leaf. So now I knew of nine such angels.

But what were they for? Obviously they were made in quantity. The stylised form suggests a tradition, while their angelic nature suggests Christmas. Since M. d'Allemagne, who lived in Paris, should have found so many, and since so few have been found elsewhere, I suspect a French origin, and this theory is supported by the *tonnelets*. The dolls are from the time of Louis XV or XVI, when the *tonnelet* was *de rigeur* for the male dancers in the court masques and ballets.

But the question still remained – for what purpose had these elaborate – and expensive – paper angels been invented? And again, Henri d'Allemagne himself provided, if not a positive answer, at least a very strong clue. In his *Histoires des Jouets*, there is a coloured engraving that I had overlooked, perhaps because it is such an old friend. It is entitled "Interiors of the Shop of a Dealer in Toys and Automata, of the 18th century." And very quaint it is, with dolls and toy ships, toy coaches and lions, all standing about in an oddly detached manner, the children in the shop looking cramped and awkward, like automatons themselves.

But my heart leapt up, as William Wordsworth's had before me, for there, balancing complacently on a tightrope slung across the shop window was one of the famous paper angels! How marvellous! Now at last I could see clearly what they had been meant for – they were balancing toys! There would have been a wire extending below the figure, with a clay ball counterweight – how odd that it doesn't show in the engraving – and if the rope were to be tilted, the angel could fly across the room.

A simple explanation, and creditable, but alas, not totally proven. The fine print of the title, which in my first excitement I had neglected to read, states, "Reconstructed after objects exhibited by M. Henri d'Allemagne." So it wasn't a real engraving, after all, but a clever pastiche by that extremely clever Frenchman and his assistant, M. Fortier-Marotte. They had apparently cut up old engravings and assembled an elaborate collage – which is why it is so convincing, yet at the same time, so disjointed. And it may explain the awkwardness of the children, for perhaps they too were really automata!

So the mystery still remains: what were the angels for? Did M. d'Allemagne have merely an inspired guess? Or did he know more than we do – did one of his angels have its balancing mechanism intact? Was he lucky enough to watch the flight of an angel, airborne again after 150 years of immobility?

One hopes so. It is enchanting to think of all those impromptu tightropes being set up, all those angels whizzing about the salons of Paris on Christmas morning. And it is amusing, too, to think of M. d'Allemagne himself, with seven or eight angels wobbling above him as he wrote. Perhaps the crude dowels and wires on my angels are original, after all. They could easily support a counterweight, and the dowel would be quite wide enough to balance on a tightrope.

And this explanation would certainly account for the many broken and missing limbs amongst the surviving angels. Even my own complete pair has bends in the legs and one very weak arm – just as though they had fallen. I wonder...

Silent Witnesses

French Court Dolls

The so-called "Court Dolls" are rare French 18th century wooden creatures with splendid court clothes, sour faces, and boldly carved genitalia. They are amongst the most potent of dolls, and as nothing is known of their origins except hearsay, the viewer is free to speculate and conjecture as to their original purpose.

I can offer my own theories about them. They were linked by two of their earliest owners – one of them a Mrs. Izole Dorgan, who owned seven of them – to the Princess Lamballe, confidante of Marie Antoinette, who was officially responsible for keeping that unhappy Queen amused. It was common knowledge that the guests at the masquerades and other entertainments staged for her Majesty by the Princess Lamballe included practised courtesans, as well as virile footmen and gardeners. These lavish parties were notorious for turning into the wildest of orgies, and indeed, it was the common knowledge of these scandalous affairs that inflamed the already smouldering hatred that the downtrodden lower classes nursed against the Queen.

But even under the most licentious of circumstances, the rigid protocol of the French Court must be

This trio from the Ardmore Public Library shows us how rich and lavish the Court Dolls are. These three were clumsily repainted a very long time ago, and this layer of alien paint is now cracking and peeling. Expert conservation could still, perhaps, save the original finish underneath.

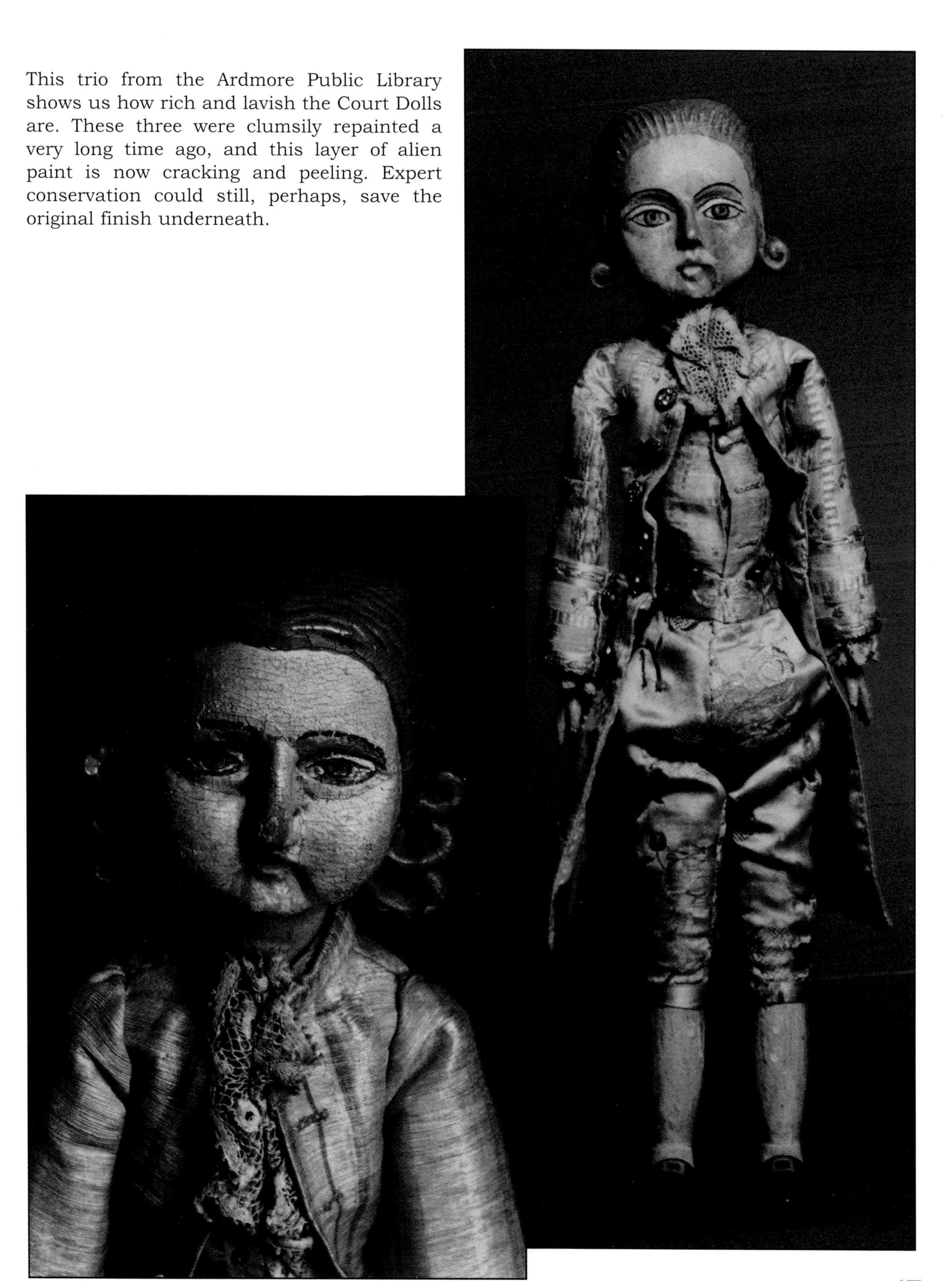

maintained. A Duchess might not befriend a gardener, and he certainly might never even speak to her! However, the dolls would have been free to flirt with whomsoever they chose, and it is my pet theory that these ill-tempered little wooden aristocrats were made available to members of the court at the Lamballe entertainments to perform such liaisons.

Although the oral traditions reported by Mrs. Dorgan proposed a total of over 40 of these curious dolls, my own researches had accounted for less than 20 of them. Lately, however, several more have surfaced.

Two of them appeared in recent doll auctions. The first one is perhaps a fake – of which there are several reputed – but not listed by me. This one's face is carved suspiciously like the child-faces of the Jumeau factory of 100 years later, and it has inset blue glass eyes, which make the similarity more pronounced. But of course, it could simply have been altered – even recarved, and the glass eyes added – over the years, and this possibility is strengthened by the fact that it possesses twin male members, similar to those of the man-doll in the red coat now in the Los Angeles County Museum.

The second doll, from the Hoyt Auction, is more convincing, although the face is still suspiciously sweet. But many of the elements ring true: the elaborate carved hair, the carved and complete body, and the stomacher with its silver thread embroidery. I have not seen this doll in person, but I think it could perhaps be a real court doll that has been played with and altered – partly redressed, too – in later years. Significantly, the auctioneers dated it circa 1825.

Learning of my interest in this subject, my old friends Stephanie and Fred Farago contacted me. The Faragos are famous for their extensive collections of Lencis and other art dolls of the post-World War I period, but their staggeringly opulent cabinets contain many other treasures. I had not realised that they possess between them three undoubtedly genuine and spectacular court dolls, acquired some time ago from auction houses.

I suspect that these are three of the superb specimens that were once in the Estelle Winthop collection. It was a great privilege for this author to see those marvellous dolls in person, for the two ladies in particular, with their wildly fashionable wooden coiffures, are amongst the finest, as well as the most extravagant of the known court dolls.

Soon after, there arrived from Paris a catalogue of Francoise Theimier's "Doll Weekend in Paris" to be held at the Hilton Hotel by the Eiffel Tower. The pride of this auction was a pair of elusive court dolls, one a gentleman and the other a hermaphrodite. I was most touched and a little saddened to discover that extensive research had been undertaken, assuming that the hermaphrodite was unique. The researchers were clearly unaware that several other hermaphroditic examples can be found in American collections, as well as dolls with other physical peculiarities.

The pair at the Parisian auction was offered in these terms: "Two rare, sexed French dolls from the 18th century which apparently belonged to the Princess de Lamballe." Again, there was that intriguing attribution, and it was claimed that they represented the scandalous "Madame la Chevaliere d'Eon and Monsieur Caron de Beaumarchais." The research, as it was presented in the catalogue, described in detail the remarkable adventures of this pair, which included espionage and duels and acts of great daring and courage, despite the fact that the Chevalier had confided to his friend Beaumarchais that he was, in fact, a woman!

This confidence did not long remain a secret, and the subsequent public speculation about the Chevalier's true gender became a very fashionable matter of wager. So rife was this scandal that the king is said to have ordered the Chevalier to wear only women's clothing until the day he/she died. As indeed, he/she did, and as Theimier records, mystery still shrouds the intriguing character of the Chevalier d'Eon.

This is all most fascinating, and I am pleased to be able to add the three closely written pages of research to my own archives of the Court of Louis XV and Marie Antionette. But the fact remains that this Court doll is not unique, and it is uncertain that any of the several existing hermaphrodites does, in fact, represent the gallant Chevalier.

The last two "new" court dolls to add to the list are very well documented. They are indeed the most exciting of the new arrivals, for they are two of the original seven described by their owner, the legendary Mrs. Dorgan, in Janet Johl's book, *The Fascinating Story of Dolls*, published such a long time ago – during the 1930s, in fact.

Their present owner, Ms. Marygray O'Brown, inherited them from her mother, who had acquired them from Mrs. Dorgan in approximately 1940, along with the famous story of the Princess Lamballe. Ms. O'Brown was good enough to send the photographs reproduced here, together with a "Studio Portrait" of the dolls taken long ago. And most exciting of all, a newspaper clipping from a Philadelphia newspaper dated March 26, 1940 – and surely the only copy now in existence – shows five of Mrs. Dorgan's seven court dolls.

Interestingly enough, one of Mrs. Dorgan's dolls was a hermaphrodite, and she too assumed that it represented the scandalous Chevalier d'Eon, being unaware that there were several other such dolls existing.

Allowing for some slight confusion and the possible appearance of the same doll in two different sets of evidence from different periods of time, I can still account for less than 30 of the 44 dolls referred to by Janet Johl. The Court Dolls remain one of the doll world's unsolved mysteries, and while I still find them – all of them – quite unlovable (if not downright sinister!) they are still, for me at least, the most fascinating of dolls.

For, as I have said in the past, I can look at the three that I am fortunate enough to own, gaze into those cold, painted eyes, and think, "That terrible Revolution is long over and done with, the protagonists long dead and their accoutrements dispersed, and there is no one left to remember that horror of horrors. But these wooden people were there. They saw the Revolution with those same painted eyes – and surely, they remember!"

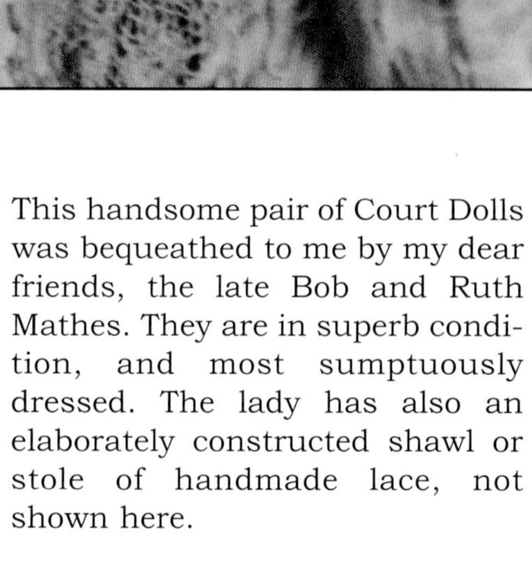

This handsome pair of Court Dolls was bequeathed to me by my dear friends, the late Bob and Ruth Mathes. They are in superb condition, and most sumptuously dressed. The lady has also an elaborately constructed shawl or stole of handmade lace, not shown here.

These companion Court Dolls were acquired from Izole Dorgan in the 1940s. Mrs. Dorgan believed that the dolls were originally owned by Princess Lamballe and played with by Marie Antionette and other adults in the French Court in circa 1776. *Collection of Marygray O' Brown.*

An engraving made from a portrait of the Princess Lamballe, which hangs in the gallery at Versailles. With her uncompromising posture, her curiously sharp features and her unyielding expression, this redoubtable lady looks – to my eyes, at any rate – startlingly like one of her own Court Dolls!

I first saw this most splendid of Court Dolls when she belonged to Kit Robbins, and again at Withington's Auction rooms, where she fetched $2,300, a lot of money at that time. I couldn't afford her then, but at a convention some time later I was offered her by a friendly dealer for $12,000, reduced from $13,000, "Since it was for me!" Needless to say I still couldn't afford her, but Estelle Johnston kindly took the photographs for me, so that I could at least have the memory! This is one of the "hermaphrodites."

This moronic-looking fellow came to me straight from an attic in New England, and he is six inches taller than all the others. There must surely have been a second, larger set of these figures, more of which may still exist, as yet undiscovered. He is the only one with a section of his head made separately. Was it perhaps meant to open to reveal a cabbage instead of a brain?

Perhaps the only Court Doll with pretensions to classic beauty, at least the only one known at present, is this elegant young lady photographed by the Mathes in the 1950s in Paris when she was still in Mme. Galea's private collection. Years later she moved from Paris to Monte Carlo, and is now in Princess Grace's Museum.

Two Court Dolls which appeared at a Paris auction in the mid-1990s. They possibly represent Madame la Chevalier d'Eon and Monsieur Caron de Beaumarchais. *Photograph courtesy François Theimer.*

This exceedingly rare carton doll from the mid-18th century is only the second example known. She is the unlikely anticedent of the simple carton dolls discussed in this chapter. *Collection of Estelle Johnston.*

Dancing in the Streets

Relics of the French Revolution

In the last chapter, we looked at the bizarre "court dolls," survivors of the last, hysterical days of the French Court just before the Revolution exploded. Only a few years later, there was another hysteria rife in Paris. Bloodlust had been let loose, anarchy had gathered force and what had begun as a high-minded, political revolt soon degenerated into an obscene holocaust.

We can find vivid depictions of this mob-fury in English literature. Dickens paints a sombre picture in his magnificent novel, *A Tale of Two Cities,* as does the Baroness Emma Orczy in her swashbuckling tale of *The Scarlet Pimpernel.* Both stories were written many years after the dreadful events had taken place, but memories are long concerning such horrors. Certainly, vivid details of those incredible times, branded on the memories of those who lived through them, have been passed down within family histories, and there is no reason to doubt them. No one, surely, would make up such things.

As always during such upheavals, there was a quick and continuous shift of power, and with power, sudden riches. Amidst all the rioting and licentiousness, there was certainly dancing in the streets; wild, uncontrolled merrymaking. Descriptions remain to us of a hideous dance called *A la Guillotine* in which the dance-steps

An all-original 18-inch carton doll dating circa 1812 with a kid body and wooden hands. Her paper and gauze clothing is glued on and her orange-red shoes are painted onto her kid feet! Her human hair wig is topped with a toque decorated with an orange feather. *Collection of Estelle Johnston.*

mimic in obscene caricature the death throes of the victims of the Revolution.

For such upstart persons of power and importance, there were always new fashions, new and wild standards of dress, diametrically opposed to what had been the costly, extravagant styles of the Royal court. The wearers of these extreme fashions received accolades which have been passed down to us, for the men were christened *Incroyables,* or "Unbelievables," whilst their even wilder women companions became known by the term *Merveilleuses*, or "Marvels."

Cruel little gimmicks of the time, worn for certain by those dancers in the streets, have been immortalised in the cartoons and caricatures of the day. For instance, one particular hairstyle, worn by both men and women, featured a knot of hair at the back of the head, but turned deliberately upwards to show the neck. It was called *A la Victime.* A popular fashion for women, at the same time, was a narrow red ribbon tied around the throat of the *Merveilleuse*, a ribbon known simply as *Ruban a la Guillotine.*

During the last war, when I was an art student busily collecting old toys whenever and wherever I could, I was offered a battered little old doll by a dealer on the Portobello

An all-original 12-1/2-inch tall carton doll, circa 1820. Her human hair wig has been braided into a crown and decorated with beads. She has a kid body with wooden hands. Her dress, straw bonnet and pink kid shoes are all pristine. *Collection of Estelle Johnston.*

Road. It was so costly and so fragile that I could not think of acquiring it, but now, how I wish that I had made the effort! For this was a doll bought in Paris from a street market stall during the days of the Revolution, almost certainly by *un Incroyable* for his dancing partner.

It was the crudest little thing. Its head and torso were made in one piece, very simply from papier-mâché. For legs, it had a single rod set into a rough, circular pedestal, and its arms were mere sticks. The dress had once been purple and crimson with much gold trim, but the remains of this finery were faded and tattered – not surprisingly, for they had been contrived from the flimsiest paper. A bedraggled green feather held down with a wisp of gold cord had once been a gay head-dress.

But the reason I should have bought this flimsy relic — and why I regret to this day that I did not — is that, painted on the doll's white throat was that sinister narrow red ribbon, the once so-fashionable *Ruban a la Guillotine*! But at that time I did not understand its significance.

I have never seen another, although the type of doll is identifiable. In Henri d'Allemagne's book, *Histories des Jouets*, published in Paris in 1903 and one of the earliest to explore our subject matter, there are plates from a distributor's catalogue of the early 19th century depicting rows of cheap, tawdry dolls, very similar to the *Merveilleuse* that I was once offered.

The interesting fact here is that the catalogue from which these plates were taken was in fact a German one, but since we know that the German toy industry already had world-wide distribution, including even to America, it is not so surprising that the cheap little Parisian street dolls should have come from Germany.

These dolls, known to collectors as "Cartons," are hard to find today. Like other "fairground" toys – the English "Bartholomew Babies" and even the celluloid "Kewpie dolls" of the 1920s, they were so flimsy and fragile that they can scarcely have lasted for more than a day or so. A few precious, battered examples do exist, still in the remains of their paper clothing, in a museum in New England, but no picture of them is currently available.

An exception is a splendid example in the collection of Estelle Johnston, which is illustrated here. The dress is contemporary with the doll, and is in good condition. It is very fine, so fine indeed that I suspect the doll to have been redressed very shortly after it was first acquired. Thus it can be said to be in "original" condition, although this is almost certainly not the costume it wore when it was originally bought.

Another exception is the bridal pair from the collection of the Strong Museum, also illustrated here. And here is a wonder, for this is a pair of "carton" dolls dressed for their wedding in the late 1790s surviving to us, miraculously untouched – perfect.

As far as I know, there are no fashion plates, engravings or paintings surviving to show us what the wedding clothes of this turbulent period would have looked like. Here once again, we find dolls mirroring mankind.

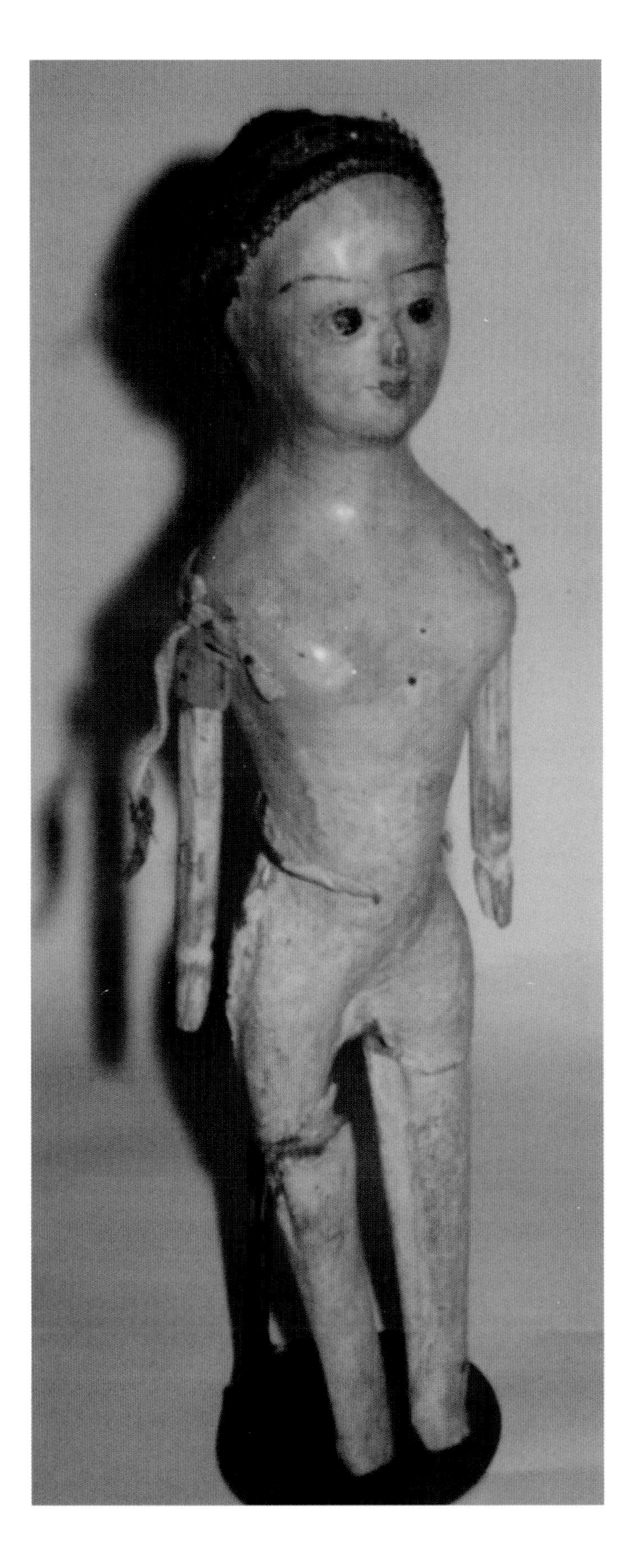

This undressed carton doll shows the structure of its body. The torso is molded down to the knees in carton. The arms are just wooden sticks attached with a bit of fabric. A wooden pole would have made her longer and would have fitted into a circular wooden base. The dress would have been longer than the doll.

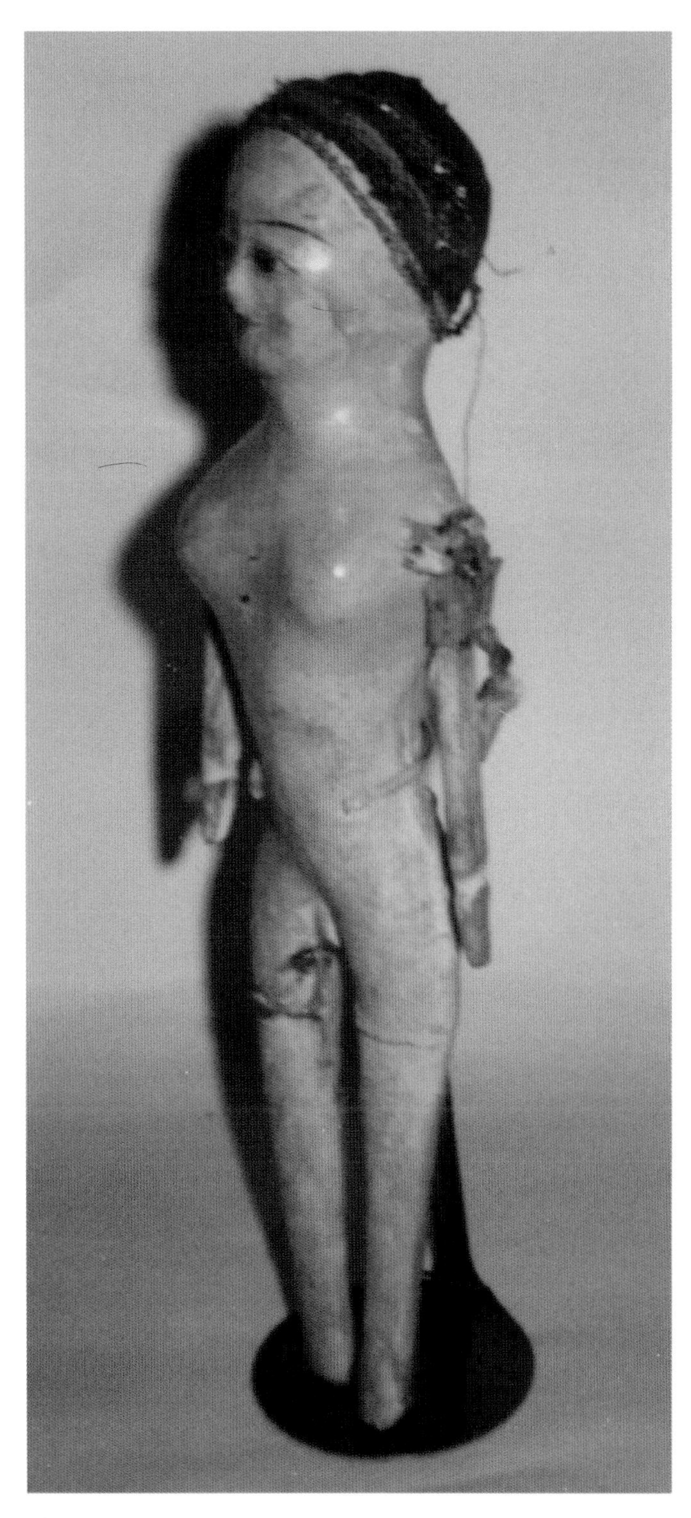

My Own D'Allemagne Dolls, The Past Revisited

In his book *Histories des Jouets*, published in Paris in 1903, Henri D'Allemagne reproduced a page from a toy maker's catalogue of almost a century before. It depicts a row of dolls, archaic, primitive, with a flamboyance very much of their period. These flimsy toys survive almost not at all, and the few specimens we have (the two in the Essex Institute, for instance) are so sadly battered as to be unrecognisable.

I have always found these vanished dolls most fascinating, and when I decided to attempt doll making, they came at once to my mind.Could I recreate their gaudy charm, the cheap, flashy brilliance so barely glimpsed in the D'Allemagne picture?

My friend Margaret Whitton unexpectedly produced a specimen, so ruinous that all clothes, limbs and even features had disappeared from its moulded cardboard body. This precious relic held nevertheless many clues, and provided the profiles from which an accurate replica could be modelled, and moulds for the *carton moulé* be made.

Equally unexpectedly, a store opened near my home in West Greenwich Village, selling fabrics from France which are printed from ancient blocks. To my delight, I could handle (and buy) cotton prints designed in the year 1810, the year of the dolls.

And so it all slowly became real, the body, the fabric, the gilt paper borders and the barnyard feathers, the "pinned-together" structure. The slickly painted features were more evidence of speedy mass-production. To acquire this ease in painting, each stroke was made only after it had been rehearsed 20 times in the air, giving to one's hand something of a facility of long practice.

The results would deceive no one. My dolls are obviously brand new and are made, in spite of all my efforts, with my own unmistakable 1970's handwriting. Nevertheless they look, I believe, very much the way the vanished dolls looked when they themselves were new, more than a century and a half ago.

A pair of carton dolls dressed for their wedding in the late 1790s. *Collection of the Strong Museum.*

From the early 19th century Maury catalogue, and reproduced in Henri D'Allemagne's epoque-making book *Histories des Jouets,* first published in 1903, a row of cheaply made "carton" dolls, from just after the French Revolution. Designed to be sold in the streets, the gaudy clothes of these frail creatures were often made of paper. It is not surprising that very few of them have come down to us.

Sense & Sensibility

The title of the famous novel by Jane Austin aptly describes the dolls that we shall examine here. They contrast greatly with the aristocratic 18th century ladies that we have already reviewed. These dolls were intended for a very different market, and they are all thoroughly commercial in concept.

The first mass-produced moulded heads of papier-mâché were introduced at the great doll-trading centre of Sonneberg, Thuringia, in the early years of the 19th century. It was a time when the long-established but insular German toy trade was expanding to embrace a world-wide market.

These early heads are outstanding. They are usually surprisingly large, beautifully modelled and conceived with great vitality, deriving in style and manner from the classical ideals of the late 18th century. These early examples have been largely neglected by collectors, simply because so few of them exist that they are virtually unknown to many people.

Most decorative objects that are in production over a long period of time have "careers" that can be divided into clearly defined stages. Examples from the first, or "pioneer" stage express new ideas and perhaps exploit new processes. They are always vivid and exciting. In the next phase, the most successful and efficient of the variants reach prominence. At this point, the objects – in this case, the dolls – acquire their distinctive characteristics and achieve the peak of their success, still fresh and original. In the third stage, the dolls become classics, and sometimes even clichés. And finally, there is decadence. The products are either drained of vitality through overproduction or they are cheapened in an effort to hold the market.

By the 1820s, our papier-mâché dolls had evolved into an economical and practical product; the body made simply and durably from two strips of stitched and stuffed kid, the wooden limbs fashioned partially by lathe. A significant feature is the hairstyle, which was moulded as one with the shoulderhead, and which thus records, faithfully, over a period of some 50 years, the sometimes astonishing vagaries of the fashions in coiffure.

The two rare and lovely ladies depicted on page 68, dating between 1810 and 1815, are especially good examples of the larger sizes, and both have the fresh, lively modelling which characterises the better dolls of this type. All have original clothing, complete and undisturbed.

The lady on the left has the formal features and the smooth, column-like neck, which are derived from classical sculpture. Her fashionable coiffure is a style based on Roman portraits. The beguilingly simple dress is printed cotton with a faded pink pattern, and the painted shoes are rose-colored. The dress with its long sleeves is perhaps a little later than the doll herself, and its very short skirt and plainly visible pantaloons suggest a young girl's costume rather than an adult's.

The lady on the right has a most unusual head with delicate, subtly modelled features. Her coiffure is graced with a braided knot, high up on the crown. The contemporary straw bonnet came with the doll, but it is oddly in conflict with the hairstyle, which requires one of the specifically designed, high-crowned bonnets of the period. This bonnet does not sit comfortably, and leads one to wonder, wistfully, if there was once a second sister doll with a different, lower hairstyle.

The dress here is of silk gauze, mounted on fine pink silk. The sash is made of the same clear pink satin ribbon as those upon the bonnet, and it is edged with the silk lace known as "blond." Again, the pantaloons suggest that this is a girl's dress. The shoes here are viridian green. Their present whereabouts are unknown, but these two ladies were once in the collection of Margaret Whitton.

The gentleman doll is very unusual. He is more difficult to date than the ladies, but was made sometime between 1810 and 1840. The distinctly child-like head with its inset glass eyes is most unusual for this period, with its distinctively painted hair, arranged *en coup-de-vent* – the proper Romantic manner. He may have been made by the Andrew Voit factory, founded in Eisfeld, Coburg, in 1806. His clothing is splendid indeed. His suit is a fashionable bottle-green colour, with large brass buttons, suggesting an earlier rather than a later date.

The careful details of his costume, the nicety of his linen and the accurate disposition of his pockets add much to the charm of this debonair young man. He possesses a towering beaver hat, which completes the correct silhouette for the Beidemeier dandy. He has clearly worn his anachronistic real gold watch-chain (revealingly known as an "Albert" in England) for a long time. In his heyday, he would of course have worn his watch on a fob, but the chain speaks clearly of affection bestowed at a later date, and one is delighted to see it left undisturbed.

These beautiful papier-mâché dolls continued to be made in great quantities until the middle of the century, and were increasingly popular to judge by the very large numbers of the later examples that have come down to us. With their small, comfortable sizes, their lightness and delicacy and their precise and intense romanticism, these dolls speak most eloquently of the tastes of their times.

There had been growing up in Europe a prosperous middle class, in which were fused the second generation of the new industrialists with the lower echelons and poor relations of the old aristocracy. The novels of Jane Austin give us telling insights into the ways of the middle class, as well as into its limitations. Her works contain no hint of the dissolute splendours of the court, or of concern with war or political crises although she was writing during one of the crucial periods of English history. Her boundaries were prescribed; she wrote for gentlefolk.

The two lady dolls, circa 1810 to 1815, are good examples of large papier-mâché dolls and both wear their original clothing. The gentleman doll dates from between 1810 and 1840 and may be from the Andrew Voit factory.

Our little dolls were intended for this middle class market, and for our next plate, a group of them has been chosen to show a panorama of the changing styles and characters of the years 1830 to 1850. In spite of great differences in mood, these dolls are above all genteel, and they invariably represent fashionable and soigné ladies and young girls.

The 1830s saw the desire for gentility and refinement reach the intensity of a cult. The inverted snobbery of dowdiness, the declaration of the vulgarity of money, and the coarseness of physical functions (even that of eating!) are brilliantly satirised in Miss Mitford's popular classic, *Cranford.* Paradoxically, this decade saw the full flowering of the romantic revival, and fashionable costumes achieved an outrageous eccentricity that was not to be matched until the early 1890s.

In the second doll from the left of our picture, these two contradictory elements meet. The coiffure with its towering loops and braids and jutting masses of curls is at the very peak of sophistication, whereas the dress is homemade and demure. The doll in the dark dress is a little earlier, and is much more restrained. The unusual head combines painted hair with real, applied curls, and the doll is serene and dignified.

By the 1840s, both the panache and the dignity were subdued, and the two examples here – the dolls at the extreme left and right of the photograph – although extremely pretty, are nevertheless abashed and self-effacing. These are perhaps the loveliest dolls in this group; their elaborate dresses are all original and undisturbed, and their calm features are as fresh as when they were first painted.

Much of the vigour and vitality had faded by the 1850s, and although the dolls of this date are plentiful, they tend to be monotonous and uninspired. The number of larger sized dolls, such as the one here in the pale dress, suggest that they no longer reflected the spirit of the age, which was neat, small, exquisite and ladylike. The smaller late doll here, in the centre of the group, is an enchanting and vivacious exception.

LEFT: A beautiful German papier-mâché from the early 1840s in mint condition, this serious and dignified doll wears unexpectedly the long clothes of a small baby. Once in my own collection, the present owner is unknown.

OPPOSITE PAGE: A most beautiful, large papier-mâché from about 1840 with inset glass eyes and a most unusual, partially applied coiffure. Papier-mâché dolls are notable for acquiring personality. This one, in her all-original costume, is vivid and even commanding – I would not be surprised to hear her speak! *Collection of Richard Wright.*

RIGHT: At first sight one might assume this to be a fairly ordinary, glass-eyed German papier-mâché doll. But gazing at her, one is slowly aware of a difference, a melting softness that is mysterious and seductive. The answer? This head is made of moulded linen! The maker is unknown and the doll is very rare. Circa 1845-50. *Collection of Richard Wright.*

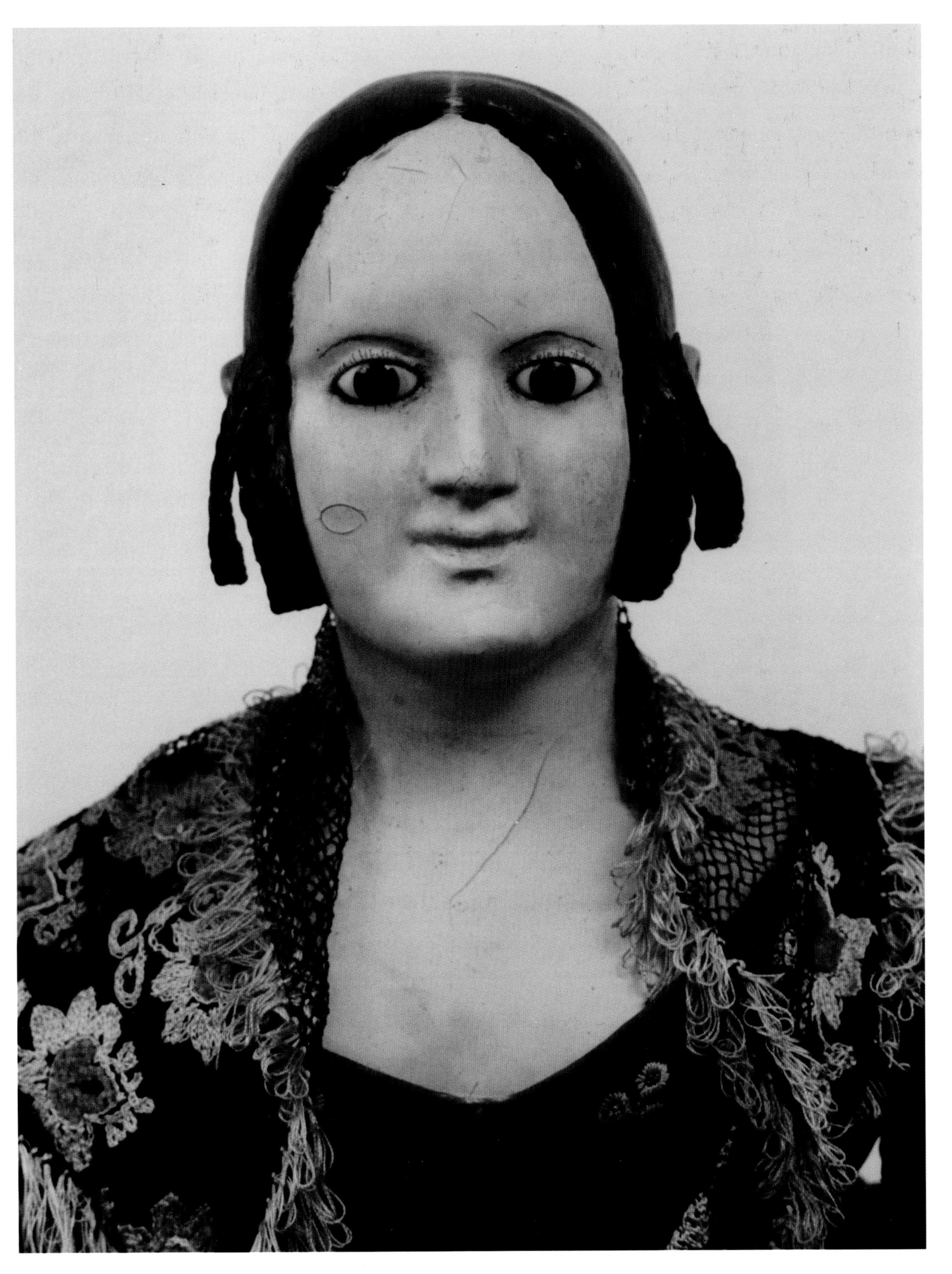

Bavarian Beauties

Even more popular (perhaps because so much cheaper) were the little wooden dolls made on much the same scale, which have been given the appropriate name, "Pegwoodens," by collectors. They are part of the enchanting microcosm formed by the toys made in the cottages of the Bavarian Alps from the late 18th century onwards.

It is a microcosm of peasant simplicity and peasant splendour, a reflection of the insular lifestyle of its creators, curiously stilted but perfectly serious, and evolved with such conviction and vivacity that it was to have an immense influence on children everywhere for over a century - including no less than Queen Victoria, who in her childhood collected, dressed and adored these little pegwooden dolls.

As late as the 1930s, this spirit was still very much alive, especially in the field of children's literature. Florence K. Upton's book, *The Adventures of Two Dutch Dolls*, and Frances Hodgson Burnett's *Racketty-Packetty House*, two nursery classics, were written in the early 1900s, and both take place in a make-believe world of wooden dolls.

H. G. Hulme Beaman's Toytown stories came later, in the 1920s, and they achieved a special immortality in Britain when they were serialised for the B.B.C.'s *Children's Hour*; they are still cherished after over 50 years of radio broadcasting. The make-believe environment created in those mountain villages so long ago is powerful indeed.

Amongst the surviving pegwooden dolls, again we find that the earliest are the finest. The wood is smooth and well seasoned, the jointing precise, and the limbs articulated with beautiful ball-and-socket joints that permit a great deal of natural movement. The initial lathe-turning is finished with careful hand carving. Faces, hair and lower limbs were painted with flat colours and then thickly varnished, giving a translucent finish that becomes mellow and beautiful with time.

The pegwoodens were cheap and plentiful, and by the 1820s had reached a level of smooth excellence that was to last until the mid-century. They were the everyday dolls for little girls on both sides of the Atlantic. The efficient processes of the craftsmen acted like a machine to standardise them; their variety and charm derive largely from the imagination and care with which they were dressed. Hundreds of little girls learned their sewing skills by making clothes for them. Kate Greenaway describes in her writings her own childish delight in the family of pegwoodens which she collected and dressed when she was small, imbuing them with life and character. And as we have already noted, the little Princess Victoria, growing up secluded and solitary in Kensington Palace, created a whole wonderland of glittering aristocrats and ballet dancers. The collection was preserved by her majesty with nostalgic care, and in her old age was presented to the British nation.

Commercially dressed pegwoodens are rare. Presumably they were such an inexpensive product that costuming of any sort was impractical. They were, however, occasionally incorporated into toys made elsewhere, while others were used to populate the fantastic little grottoes of shells and minerals, which, under their glass domes, were popular parlour ornaments in the early 19th century.

In a Superior Class

Most of the pegwoodens that have come down to us are in the small sizes, dolls comfortable in a child's hands, like the ones so loved by Princess Victoria. Especially popular, it seems, were the 5- - to 6-inch ones, perhaps since they made perfect denizens for the new commercially made dolls' houses, which had almost entirely replaced the larger, more opulent baby houses of previous generations.

But amongst the earlier pegwoodens, we find a few very rare and very large examples, so rare as to imply that very few of them were made, perhaps because they were of necessity much more expensive, and in a superior class by themselves. They are always full of character, dignified and gracious, very reminiscent of Jane Austin's heroines!

The first doll to consider here is a 40-inch marvel dated about 1815, from the Schott collection, now in the Santa Barbara Museum of Fine Art. Apart from her unusual size, this doll is spectacular, from her finely carved coiffure to the tips of her slippers. She is perhaps unique, and certainly as rare as hen's teeth. Everything about her is original and pristine. Her head is carved with such great sensitivity that it might have been taken from life. This is one of the rare and desirable pegwoodens that can boast of a carved and painted chemise neckline, this one painted with a formal garland of flowers. The neckline of the original "round gown," so fashionable at that time, had been carefully adapted to display this decoration.

From my own collection comes a much smaller and slightly later pegwooden, from about 1810 to 1812, also from the rarefied group with ornamental, chemise necklines. Here, the decoration is a romantic garland of leaves and roses. Again, a round gown, this one made of gauze with a woven pattern, is cut to display this ravishing conceit. By great good fortune, the striped silk shawl, which so perfectly sets off the costume, has survived intact. The hairstyle here is piquant and unusual, and altogether, the doll has a summery freshness and vitality that enchants everyone who sees her.

A third large and very unusual pegwooden is from the personal collection of Richard Wright, the legendary dealer and television personality. Richard is a beloved friend of many years standing, and it is always a joy to visit him. Not the least of my delights, besides the pleasure of browsing through his Aladdin's cave of a shop, is the privilege – not extended to everyone – of seeing his own, very private collection. It is, as one might imagine, a very select assemblage of the rarest of the rare.

Richard's doll is another very large one, 38 or 40 inches tall. She is later by perhaps ten years than the two we have just discussed, and slightly more sophisticated. Again, this one is carved with great sensitivity, almost certainly from a live model. Here is another beautiful coiffure, and this one has a delicious, special feature. The tuck-comb in her high Grecian knot is carved separately, and is removable, and once upon a time the doll would have owned a changeable selection of hair ornaments – including, perhaps, a knot of carved wooden flowers?

Here again, everything is pristine and perfect – so much so that first-time viewers are likely to exclaim, "What a pity she's been redressed!" But she hasn't. The lovely, blue striped calico gown, fuller in the skirt and lower waisted than the Schott doll's dress, is original to the doll. What providence can have preserved this lovely creature, safe and immaculate through time and travel to Pennsylvania, I cannot imagine. But looking at her, I am profoundly grateful that it did so.

Pegwooden doll with carved and painted chemise, Bavarian, circa 1815. This magnificent wooden is from the Schott Collection.

My own smaller and slightly later example, with her garland of leaves and roses, together with two other very early and desirable pegwoodens.

Richard Wright's wonderful big wooden doll.

A large and very early pegwooden with elaborate carving and construction. This wonderful doll boasts of a swivel-jointed waist and a removable comb in her hair. She also has the rare and so enviable carved and decorated neckline. *Collection of Estelle Johnston.*

Another view of the larger pegwooden doll pictured on page 75.

Dolls made from organic materials (such as wood, rubber, gutta percha, and rawhide) acquire aesthetic virtues of their own. This doll has a head made of rubber in a pale sand color. The features and the simple arranged hair are sensitively modeled, and the restrained, stylized coloring enhances the delicate features. When the rubber was new it was soft and pliant, but today with the natural hardening and shrinking, the doll has acquired a static quality, a monumental serenity that finds echoes in the simplicity of her dress. Made at home in the 1870s, the woolen dress with its velvet trim now has a rubbed patina that complements the finely weathered surface of the ancient rubber. *Coleman Collection.*

Very little is known of this glorious, early German pegwooden, but it is surely from a most superior manufacturer. Dressed with care and at considerable expense, it must have been a "best" doll since it has come down in such perfect condition. *Collection of Estelle Johnston.*

Harlequin in the Nursery

Most of us, I think, assume that the concept of dolls for boys is a recent phenomenon, starting with the runaway success of GI Joe some 20 years ago and followed closely by the equally popular Outdoor Men and Star Wars characters, the Bionic pair, and then a host of space-oriented heroes, all too numerous to list here, but all quite eligible as dolls for boys.

But a quick delve into history will show us that this is not true. In fact, there were many commercial dolls available to boys, in Europe at least, for most of the 19th century. Not little girl dolls, of course. But many engravings and book illustrations of those years will show, right alongside his sister with her familiar wax or papier-mâché treasure, a boy in pantaloons happily clutching his soldier or sailor, his Harlequin or his Punchinello, a dressed figure almost as big as himself that could only be classified as a doll, albeit a doll intended for a boy to play with.

During the first half of the 19th century, the Harlequins, those supermen of their day, were popular, and the Punchinellos, the "top-dogs," even more so. The reason is not hard to find. The itinerant *Commedia* or *Kasperl* theatre of the streets was a common traditional entertainment in most European countries, and certainly in France, Germany and Italy. It had its equivalent in England in the "Punch and Judy" show.

In Paris, on New Year's Day, the tough little boy here, is clutching his new "Punchinello" doll, almost as big as himself! Hand-colored engraving, circa 1815.

The new fashionable health cure at that time was sea bathing, and seaside holidays were becoming very popular amongst all classes. By the end of the second decade, those historic little street theatres had found new homes right on the sands. With the crude, knock-about natures of their characters and the outrageous brutality of the plots, these outdoor performances appealed especially to the little boys. And thanks to the toyshop, they could all have a Punchinello or a Harlequin, a Kasperl or a Mr. Punch of their very own. Many of them survive to this day.

Amongst the plethora of papier-mâché-headed dolls produced in the Bavarian Alps in the early 19th century, there are many wonderful men, often with moulded hats and headgear. At least some of these, the splendid, strutting soldiers, for instance, with their accurately rendered uniforms and their brave helmets and shakos rendered in the moulded papier-mâché were surely put out with little boys in mind.

I wish I had the leisure and the means nowadays for intensive research, for I find this paradox fascinating. Surely, for instance, the commemorative dolls made to celebrate national heroes – especially in England – were made for boys to cherish. And I myself possess a fierce, commanding little wax man-doll that was the personal boyhood treasure of an equally fierce, domineering American Colonel. Until he died it sat proudly on his desk, and might not be touched by anyone!

So when and where did this tradition come to an end? For by the time that I was growing up in London, in the 1920s and 30s, dolls for boys were unheard of Teddy bears and other animal toys, yes, but never a doll! I believe the change came about abruptly in 1896, when the scandalous trial of Oscar Wilde rocked English Society to its core.

In these permissive days, it is hard to remember that the Victorian social world was indeed very prim and proper, and that aberrations of the slightest kind were not only scandalous, they were invisible. Queen Victoria herself declared that she did not believe any such thing actually existed. But when the nine-day's wonder of the Wilde trial was over, there was left behind an anxious nurturing of the masculine image, an implacable emphasis on virility. And dolls for boys disappeared overnight.

This universal stricture was not relaxed until the 1960s, when the advent the "flower-children" heralded a worldwide revolution of the young. That is the climate that ushered onto the scene GI Joe and all his muscular followers. Today, those first plastic boys' dolls have become very collectible. I even have some of the more colourful ones – the Star Wars dolls, for example – on my own shelves.

But, old romantic that I am, it is the earlier, more heroic boys' dolls that really win my heart: those vivid Harlequins and vibrant Punchinellos, to say nothing of the dashing Hussars and Highlanders. How those little boys of so long ago must have loved them! How proudly those very masculine playthings must have been paraded for the pleasure and the envy of less fortunate boys! These were dolls to hold the confidences, the dreams and the aspirations of those young heroes-in-the-making, just as the wide-eyed little girl dolls and the stately, wise lady dolls shared the secret wishes and imaginings of their sisters.

These venerable fellows, some of them by now 150 years old and more, are the boys' dolls that capture my own imagination, that keep me endlessly fascinated.

A very special, early German china doll, the glazed boy's head and lower limbs being mounted on an articulated, wooden body. His very fashionable costume of about 1830 is for a young teenager, original and in such perfect condition as to imply a "best" doll, to be looked at on special occasions but never to be played with. *Collection of Dorothy Dixon.*

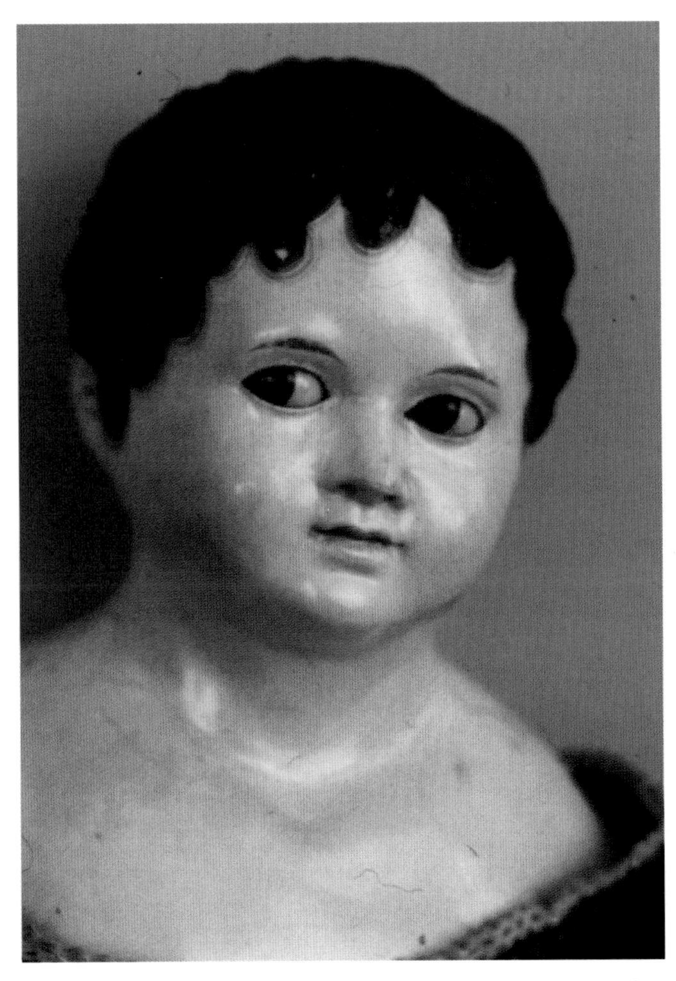

A rare, German, flirty-eyed papier-mâché boy doll from the 1840s. He is particularly cunning, and if he did indeed belong to a little boy as well as he may have he could have led his owner into all sort of mischief. *Collection of Dorothy Dixon.*

How delighted and proud some lucky little boy (a German, perhaps?) must have been to find this big soldier doll waiting under his tree one Christmas morning in the 1850s. Decked out in his officer's uniform, here was a future comrade and partner in all sorts of adventures. *Collection of Richard Wright.*

A German flirty-eyed papier-mâché pair from the 1840s. *Collection of Dorothy Dixon.*

Surely planned with little boys in mind, this debonair papier-mâché soldier, with his cap modelled in one piece with his head, is dressed as an officer with much soutache braid. *Collection of Michael Canadas.*

OPPOSITE PAGE: I was so pleased to be introduced to this early German papier-mâché doll, at first because of his dashing Scottish officer's uniform, complete with kilt and sporran, and all as fresh as if it had been made yesterday. But I became truly excited when I read the note that has been with him for all these years. In beautiful copperplate it says: "For Alfred. Brought by his Mama from Scotland." *Collection of Michael Canadas.*

For Alfred
Brought by his Mamma
From Scotland

As handsome a devil as any lady doll might swoon over, this fellow with his rare, rare bisque head by Dehors sports a moustache that is moulded as well as painted. "Love's young dream" he certainly was, but he might also very well have been some lucky little boy's best friend and confidante. *Collection of Michael Canadas.*

A charming Victorian card, depicting a little boy awakening on Christmas morning to find his new Punchinello doll. Marcus Ward, circa 1875. (At this time, the color of the ribbons had as yet no significance, pink being deemed a becoming color for such a blonde child.)

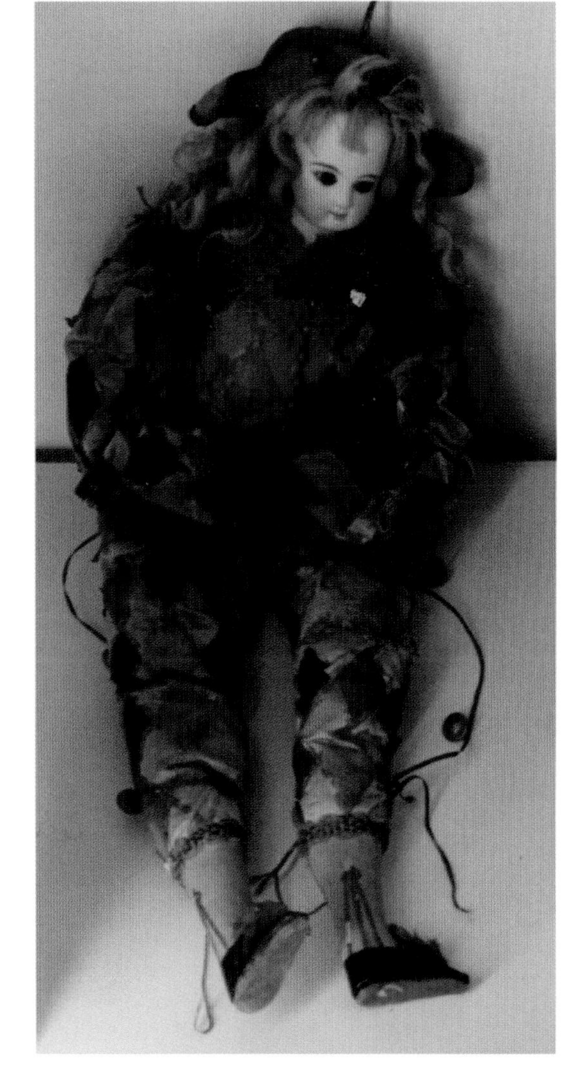

This extravagant Harlequin marionette with a French bisque head was almost certainly intended as a boy's toy. *Collection of the Strong Museum.*

Dolls decorated for Christmas and brought out to be added to, year after year, until they become family treasures, seems to have been a Yankee tradition. I have seen a number of girl's dolls decorated in this way, but never before such a doll intended for a boy. This large, dreamy-eyed, German papier-mâché lad is the exception. Warmly dressed for the snow in the late 1840s or early 1850s, he was bedecked with all sorts of boy's toys, year after year. (In the 1890s someone added an incongruous little girl's doll, which I'm sure he wishes away!) *Collection of Richard Wright.*

Parlour Ornaments

Amongst the many different dolls and toys that survive to us from the first half of the 19th century, there are to be found a great number of pretty objects preserved, either in shadowboxes or else beneath the ubiquitous glass domes or "shades," as they were called at the time. They served as parlour ornaments, of course, taking their places amongst all the decorative clutter that was thought to be indispensable to a fashionable drawing room.

All sorts of dolls are to be found thus preserved, some in such quantities as to comprise categories. Dolls dressed as peddlers, for instance, either singly or in pairs of a man and a woman, were apparently very popular, judging by the numbers that survive. Curiously primitive dolls, dressed fantastically in shellwork, are also to be found in great numbers, together with miniature scenes — rustic landscapes, market stalls, even church interiors, all peopled with carefully dressed little dolls.

The origin of this fashion lies in the rise of the middle classes, virtually all over Europe, during those early years of the 19th century. The debilitating wars that ransacked whole countries, together with the progress, almost unnoticed, of the insidious industrial revolution, had created new riches, and new power. The old aristocracy had been very sure of itself, the new ones had to prove themselves, and one of the distinguishing characteristics of this new class was its devotion to refinement of behaviour and of outlook. Significantly, such words as "Genteel" and "Ladylike" began to be used at this time.

It was in these early years of the new century that "Schools for Young Ladies" made their appearance, together with the even more desirable "Finishing Schools" abroad. Only the well-to-do could send their daughters to such expensive establishments, where they learned to speak French and Italian, to sing and to play the harp and the pianoforte, to draw, to paint and embroider. And of course, they learned proper deportment and manners.

The watercolours and the needlework they brought back home with them were hung proudly in the parlour as status symbols, and were eagerly copied by less fortunate young ladies. The presence in the parlour of a sampler, a silk picture or a bouquet of wax flowers under a glass shade implied ease and refinement. This I am sure, is the origin of the popularity of home-made "parlour ornaments."

Such things vary in quality, of course, depending a great deal upon the skill, and even more on the imagination, of their creators. But the best of them are enchanting, as, for instance, is the pair of peddler dolls depicted opposite, which date from about 1825.

These are our familiar pegwoodens, although they have "alien," paper mâché heads. Only eight inches high, they were dressed at home — or at school — with great seriousness and realism. One is sure that the maker was familiar with the traditional peddlers who, in the early 19th century, were still welcome visitors to the countryside, bringing to the farmhouses and cottages their portable wares, simple enough, but perhaps not readily available in rural districts.

The man doll opposite, with his endearing fringe of whiskers, offers a large tray of such goods, while his wife, in her classic red cloak, carries a capacious basket. Their goods include such ambitious objects as an inlaid workbox, a chessboard, a tiny dolls' house and a pair of candlesnuffers. Incredibly, all these minute objects have been fashioned, with both skill and dexterity, from paper — a minor, decorative masterpiece!

The second peddler here is a commercial one, some 20 years later than the first pair. This is a much taller doll, nearly a foot high, but this again is a pegwooden with an alien head. It is very beautiful, grave and dignified, with a smooth, classical coiffure, more suited to a lady, one would have thought, than to an itinerant peddler woman. Again, she is warmly and appropriately clad, and her basket contains such bewitching objects as a paper of tiny straight pins, a card of equally minuscule buttons, a fine comb and a toothbrush. Not to be ignored, either, is the pair of "jet" bracelets and the many perfectly knitted objects, as well as

English Peddler dolls, their wares all home-made. circa 1825.

the absurd, mock-ermine tippet. This doll's present whereabouts are unknown.

Most of the shell-dressed dolls to be found have a similar — and very interesting — origin, for they come from the coast of Brittany, and are among the first seaside souvenirs. Seabathing, so heartily recommended by doctors in the late 18th century, had made seaside holidays fashionable by the time the first commercially made shell dolls appeared. These early examples are notable for their vitality; I suspect that their makers were the wives and daughters of the local fishermen, and they are imaginative and idiosyncratic.

Often, "boughten" doll's heads were attached to homemade bodies, but the pair illustrated opposite, bottom, are handsome pegwoodens, mounted on circular bases of pinewood. They wear peasant costumes, and the shells have been assembled on bases of green paper, heavily varnished, while a red wax was used to attach them. The effect is very rich, although the shells are sometimes absurdly large. The choice is very limited, suggesting that the shells were all obtained locally. Perhaps these were indeed the products of a small, cottage industry. A fisherman's daughters could very well have made them to sell, just as they sold their knitting.

The most spectacular — and enviable — shell doll it has ever been my good fortune to see is also depicted here, on page 97. Again this is a pegwooden, dressed as a fine lady of about 1820. The shellwork here is carried out in the tiny (black) shells quite common to the northern French coast — I have seen whole beaches composed of them. But this lucky doll sports a collar, a head-dress, a reticule, stockings and a long, draped stole of what appears at first to be some sort of lace. It is with disbelief, compounded with admiration for the fortitude of the creator, that one learns that this intriguing substance is dried skin from the underbellies of lizards!

Repressing a shudder, I turn to a most romantic parlour ornament for another example. On page 96 is a wedding souvenir from New England, a pair of papier mâché-headed dolls representing a Quaker bride and groom. Judging by the costumes, this is an early group dating from 1810 to 1815. They are dressed surprisingly in cornhusks, the earliest such dolls that I have ever seen. They are endearingly serious, and their costuming was carried out with great care. It was clearly a summer wedding, and the man's broad-brimmed hat must have been a straw one. Over their painted hair, they each have wigs made of cornsilk.

She does not carry a bouquet, but a little basket, full of corn-blossom, and her wide poke bonnet has a wreath of these flowers, as does his straw hat. This is altogether a most charming parlour ornament, and how grateful I am for the glass shade, which has kept it in almost pristine condition for nearly 200 years.

One last detail should not be overlooked. In the right-hand pocket of his coat is a scroll of cornhusk, to represent his marriage lines!

ABOVE: A commercial peddler, circa 1845, is almost a foot high. Her basket contains tiny straight pins, buttons, a comb and a toothbrush.

Early Shell dolls from Brittany, circa 1830.

A rare early wedding souvenir dating about 1805-1810. These are classic German papier-mache dolls with the stiff leather bodies and wooden limbs. They have been dressed in cornhusks, very unusual for such an early date. They are Plainfolk, perhaps Quakers, but it is interesting to note that they both have long hair, contrived from cornsilk, down to their shoulders. Both their hats are wreathed in flowers (cornseeds) and she carries a basket of similar flowers. The rolled document in his pocket is their marriage lines. *Author's collection.*

LEFT: A very early tuck comb pedlar doll. *Collection of Estelle Johnston.*

A 6-1/2-inch jointed wooden doll dressed in an 1820's style outfit made of tiny black shells. The head covering, upper sleeves, collar and reticule are made of lizard underbelly!
Collecton of Estelle Johnston.

LEFT: A small tuck comb doll presides over a bazaar table covered with tiny accessories. *Collection of Estelle Johnston.*

A charming family of papier-mâché pedlars. The boys, circa 1830, came from the collection of Mrs. DeWitt Clinton Cohen. The lady is slightly later. Author's collection.

American Primitive

The dolls in this chapter were made by Izannah Walker, a spinster who lived in Central Falls, Rhode Island during the second and third quarters of the 19th century. There is good reason to believe that they were the first original, commercial dolls ever made in America. Because of their great beauty, as well as their extraordinary background, it was decided to give them a chapter to themselves.

Tantalisingly little is known about the maker of these American primitives, and what is known is mostly hearsay, elaborated on the statements of a grandniece, Mrs. Norman Robertson. Family recollections are notoriously elastic, and Mrs. Robertson's fascinating accounts, which seem to have been handed down from her mother, are richly descriptive, but often puzzlingly inconsistent when it comes to the facts. For instance, she gives four different dates for the completion of the first dolls, and two different death dates for Izannah Walker.

Although her factual evidence seems cloudy and unreliable, Mrs. Robertson's family history is nevertheless invaluable in that it provides us with a very vivid impression of Izannah Walker herself. She was clearly a remarkable character. According to Mrs. Robertson's account, which was published in a Rhode Island newspaper, "Aunt Izannah always deplored the fact that she was not a man. However, she made dolls and dolls' furniture, tinkered with household gadgets, designed a parlour heater that 'beat Ben Franklin's,' raised her canaries, dabbled in real estate, and was looked upon with admiration by her contemporaries because of her skill with carpenter's tools, so perhaps she was resigned."

Izannah Walker was born, according to Mrs. Robertson, in 1817, and she began making her dolls in the 1840s, but it was not until the summer of 1873 that they were patented as "rag dolls."

Their heads, which are painted with oil colours, are charmingly simple and primitive looking, although they are surprisingly complicated in design. Layers of glued cloth were pressed between two pairs of dies for both the front and the back of the head. When the shells so formed were dry and hard, they were covered with a layer of cotton batting and then with pasted stockinette, after which they were replaced between the dies and pressed again.

The resultant forms were stitched and glued together, and the head was ready to be stuffed and painted. The padded layer acts as a buffer that protects the painted surface. It also gives the heads their curious vibrancy, since the top surface is yielding, like a child's firm flesh. It is this secondary layering process that is protected by the 1873 patent.

Such a doll was not invented overnight, and Mrs. Robinson tells of the struggles to perfect the layering process, including an amusing story of the long wrestle with the problem of keeping the surface of the stockinette just stiff enough to hold the paint without cracking. This problem was solved abruptly when Aunt Izannah, in bed one night, sat up suddenly to hear a voice commanding, ex cathedra, "Use paste!"

However, as the Colemans gently point out in their entry on the Walker dolls in their *Collectors' Encyclopedia of Dolls*, to be legally valid, a patent claim must be made for a product within two years of its appearance on the market. And this means that the Walker dolls could not have been for sale publicly before 1871.

This is considerably different from the date the family gives, and although such discrepancies are common amongst family histories, 30 years is too disquieting a difference to ignore. In the absence of further facts, we turn to the dolls themselves to seek the explanation.

All the Walker dolls that survive to us are smooth and competently made, and their elaborate structure was certainly not evolved overnight. There must surely have been long and discouraging trial and error periods, as well as many other voices in the night before the beautiful dolls that we know today were perfected. Thus, Izannah could well have been making dolls in the 1840s – which were not exactly the dolls with which we are so familiar. Also, one must remember that Central Falls, Rhode Island, in the mid-19th century, was no metropolis. The eccentric Miss Walker might well have perfected her dolls and sold them at her church bazaar and to friends and neighbours long before anyone took them seriously enough to encourage her to patent them.

There is a third explanation for the time discrepancy, if the first two seem too weak to be valid. Dies were – indeed, still are – quite expensive things to have custom-made. Yet Izannah had several sets, as can be seen by the variety of dolls depicted here. These dies would have had to be made early in the dolls' careers, judging from their style, and it is perfectly plausible that she would not have thought it necessary to change or update them. Children's toys have a tendency to ossify and become classic. There were, for instance, china

This group of Izannah's dolls shows some of the different molds used by the artist over the years. When photographed they were in the collection of Maurine Popp.

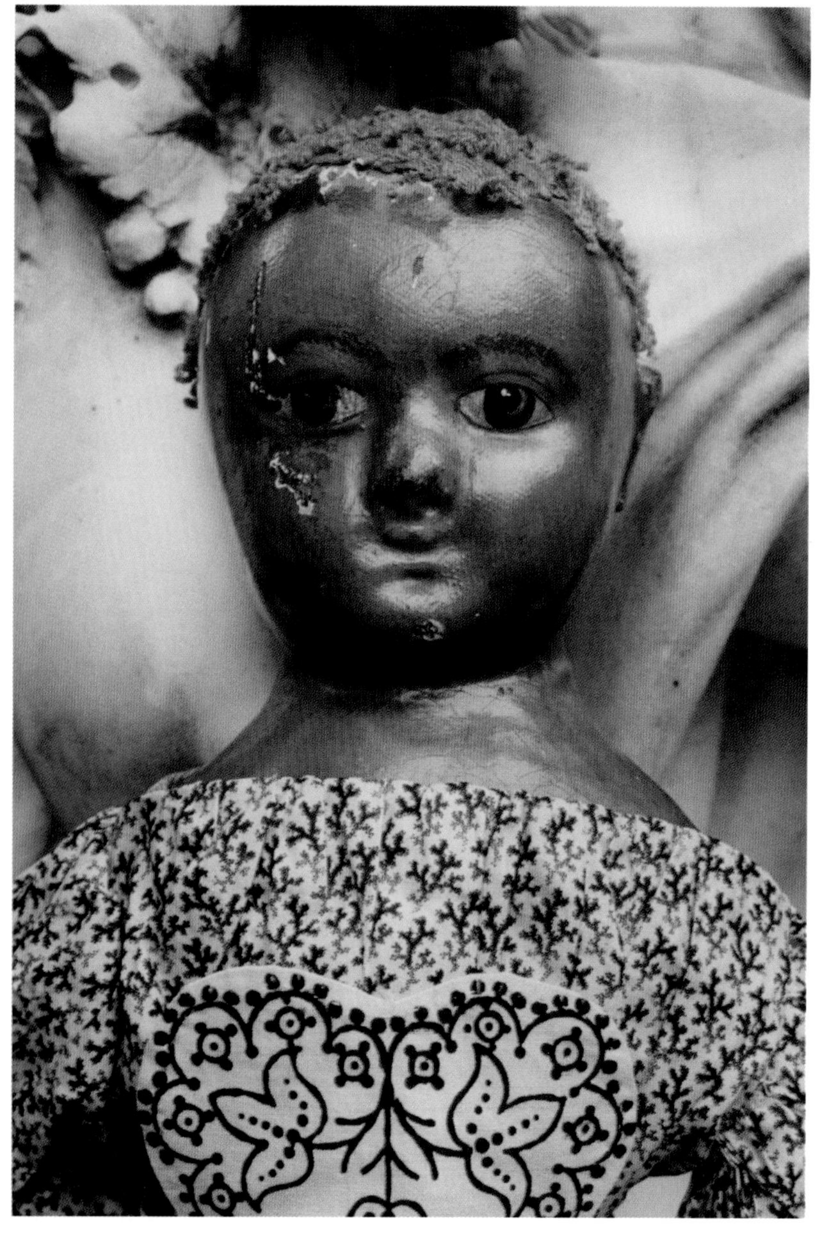

All original and wearing its original dress, this black Izannah Walker is as rare as hen's teeth! *Collection of Richard Wright.*

dolls and wooden toys produced in Germany, unchanged for at least 60 years, and which were accepted without question by shopkeepers and purchasers alike.

To Americans today, the Walker heads recall the style and character of the 1840s, but we must remember that our ideas of any 19th century period are based on the styles of Paris and London. Even smart New Yorkers used to feel that their Paris dresses were too outré to wear on Fifth Avenue, and would put them away for two years until New York had "caught up."

Central Falls, as we have suggested, was not a very sophisticated place, and in the 1870s there were doubtless many little girls, both there and in similar small towns, whose clothes and hairstyles resembled those of the Walker dolls enough for the dolls to be acceptable, if not the last word in style. So it could well be that many of the Walker dolls that survived today were produced as late as 1870, from dies that were made ten or even 20 years earlier.

The group of 8 Izannahs on page 101 shows some of the different moulds used over the years. The bodies are as varied as the faces: the hands and feet are hand-modelled and hand-stitched, as are their delicate, applied ears. The lower limbs are beautifully painted; some dolls have bare feet with deftly stitched toes and others have shoes with painted laces. There is an unsubstantiated theory among collectors that the bare feet are earlier, and it has been confirmed by one experienced collector that she has never found a doll with the patent label that also has bare feet.

The two dolls in the bottom left-hand corner have the patent label, proving that they were made after 1873. They shake our theories, so confidently stated earlier, for they are quite different from all the other dolls. The modelling is vaguer, the eyes are painted with insistence but with less assurance, and there is a conscious striving after naturalness.

As so often happens, when we try rationally to solve enigmas, the dolls themselves, bland and serene, confound us!

An original Izannah Walker doll holds three miniature versions made by Meriel Marlar. The doll in front belongs to *Caroline Edleman*, all the others are from the *Carol Corson Collection*.

These wonderful dolls have always been scarce, and throughout the decades, since the earliest collectors discovered them, attempts have been made to reproduce them, but with no success. Oh, quite a number of artists have succeeded in copying the superficial appearance – the "Early American" look with the simple, corkscrew hairstyle and the low-necked, calico dresses. But no one, to my knowledge at least, has succeeded in reproducing Izannah's complicated processes by which she produced that startlingly lifelike, tactile quality which is unique to her work. No one, that is, until my dear friend, Meriel Marlar, took up the challenge.

Meriel appears to be an English girl, both by her accent and by her habits (Like me, she has to have tea at four o'clock every day, or her world falls apart!) Meriel has for many years now worked with Richard Wright, and her studio is at the top of his magical shop in Birchrunville, Pennsylvania. It is an equally magical lair from which most visitors are strictly forbidden, and it is one of my favourite of all places.

I have many times declared in print my belief that Meriel is a witch – a declaration which she receives with laconic indifference – for her skills as a restorer of antique toys are positively uncanny. I possess, for instance, a fine, early wooden "Grodnerthal," complete and, apparently, perfect in all its original clothes. However, one entire arm and one leg from the knee-joint down were once missing and were replaced, years ago, by Meriel. But the records of this restoration have been lost, and now no one, not even Meriel herself, can be sure which are the restored limbs and which the original. But when her work is so perfect, does it matter?

Meriel has always loved the Izannah Walker dolls, and for years now, she has been the only person capable of perfect restorations to these rare – and quite fragile – treasures, especially their hands and feet, which are their most vulnerable parts. Some time ago, she decided to take up the challenge to make a complete and original Izannah Walker-type doll – not, heaven forbid, as a fake, but rather as a tribute to a beloved and reverenced artist. She decided, first of all, to use a scale never used by the New England artist, six inches high. The first dolls she made were triumphs, perfect and beautiful enough to have pleased Izannah herself. But they were unmistakably in Meriel's "handwriting," with their own, indefinable "look."

Encouraged, Meriel went on to explore other possibilities. Black Izannahs are super-rare, and this was Meriel's next endeavour. She made only two of them, and very wonderful they are. Finally, she created a version with oriental features and skin colouring, something that does not exist amongst the old Walker dolls. And these are my personal favourites, serious and dignified, and quite unlike anything ever made before.

There are not many of Meriel's little masterpieces in existence, and there may never be any more. "They are so time consuming," she said. "And once I knew I could make them successfully, the impetus was gone. I can quite understand why Izannah herself, busy as a beaver running her business – besides trying to run the small Rhode Island town she lived in – should have had no time to make more than a few every year." So here we have an enchanting paradox, where the new dolls are more scarce and, to some of us, more desirable than the old!

Romantic Revival

The atmosphere of the 1840s is a curiously complex one, and it is not easy to define in concise terms. In contrast with the proceeding decades, the 1840s are subdued and dove-colored. There is a sense of determined domesticity, of retrenchment, of taking the time to consolidate new powers, or to recoup recent losses. The newly-wed Queen Victoria of England became the symbol of this decade, and indeed, she spent it most domestically, filling her palaces with nurseries. It was into this quiet, rather dowdy atmosphere which pervaded most of Western Europe that the early porcelain dolls made their debut.

The beginnings of the commercial china dolls, which are such typical, mid-19th century objects, are surprisingly vague. Little is known for certain, and we can only point to the dolls as they appear on the scene. During the 1840s we find a number of superb porcelain heads, mostly with beautiful, matching limbs. Often unmarked, they are works of the highest order. On the rare occasions when the factory can be identified, we are not surprised to find it is a famous one. The Royal Berlin Porcelain Factory as well as the Royal Factory of Copenhagen made a wide variety of dolls that are clearly marked. There are several other distinguishable manufacturers and one hopes that research will in time shed more light on them.

A German china head doll from the 1840s with a rare hairstyle. About 24-inches tall, she came with a big wardrobe of clothing. *Collection of Richard Wright.*

An extremely rare "JP" china head doll made by the French firm Jacob Petit. It dates from about 1840. *Collection of Richard Wright.*

A group of K.P.M. (Koenigliche Porzellan Manufactur) brown-haired china head dolls. Approximately 20-22-inches tall, all are from the 1840s and all are wearing all-original clothes. *Collection of Richard Wright.*

A German wax over papier-mâché boy doll, circa 1865. Similar dolls in this kind of case are found in European churches as memorials to deceased children. *Coleman Collection.*

Love in Wax

In our first chapter, we glanced at some of the lovely 18th century wax church figures that have survived to us, and in our second, we spoke of some fine wax dolls from that same period, which were clearly from the same sources. We observed that these dolls were sidelines of wax-workers whose main output was of religious figures.

Progressing into the 19th century, we find wax-workers enjoying a new wave of prosperity, since decorative objects made of wax became increasingly fashionable during the first half of the century. Groups of figures, miniature scenes in cases and baskets of luscious fruit or delicate flowers were all made professionally in large quantities, both in England and on the Continent. These good times were, alas, to be short-lived. Soon a good deal of that trade was destroyed by amateur competition, as wax working became a more and more popular parlour employment.

There were, of course, steady requests for waxen wreaths for graves, and in Catholic countries there was still a demand for religious work. It is not too outrageous to assume, however, that the vast variety of wax dolls that appeared from the 1840s onward was directly related to the diminishing demand for other wax artifacts, and to the needs of the workers for other sources of income. In this context, it is significant that some of the best of the early English wax doll makers – Montenari, for instance, and Pierotti – were Italian immigrants.

Wax seems an unlikely and impractical material to choose for doll making, although the results can be ravishingly pretty. There is a factor of impermanence involved here, and it is significant to note that the dolls made of durable materials, such as wood, composition or papier-mâché were now fairly cheap. The expensive – and thus fashionable and desirable – dolls were the fragile ones, top-heavy and very breakable Chinas, thin brittle bisques and friable wax.

Wax is essentially an organic material, and it has its own aesthetic qualities. It is exceptionally elastic, with a large range of surface tension. It is capable of imitating widely different textures, especially organic ones – rough-pored leaves, soft shining fruit, a child's velvety skin – all can be simulated in wax so as to deceive the eye.

Wax dolls can be divided conveniently into two main categories that are quite different in origin and effect. The first division should properly be described as *waxed* dolls, since they have in fact composition or papier-mâché heads that have been dipped in wax to give them a richer finish. This is in contrast with the second group, in which the wax itself is the basic material, and is poured into the mould.

The waxed dolls make an early enough appearance (the first quarter of the 19th century) to have been amongst the new ideas of the rapidly expanding German toy industry. They derive from toy-makers crafts rather than from the ancient art of wax working. In fact, they have a good deal in common with the old German wooden toys; like them, their heads are modelled simply, with jovial, toy-like faces. There is little to distinguish one doll from another. But they are quaint and charming, and with their highly stylised concept, they are very redolent of the spirit of their times.

The poured-wax doll is entirely different, both in structure and in effect. Eclipsed for a while by the flood of commercial dolls that appeared on the market in the 1820s and 1830s, the beautiful products of the traditional wax-workers had largely vanished from the major markets. It is not until the 1850s that we find ambitious – and expensive – new wax dolls appearing to put new life into that ancient trade. These were the poured waxes, the best of which, during the next 20 years, achieved a high degree of accomplishment. They were made apparently without thought of cost, secure in the knowledge that these were indeed luxury items, fit toys even for the children of royalties all over Europe.

No expense was spared for these pampered darlings. Their inset glass eyes were the finest available and their wigs were often of human hair, set directly into the wax in small groups or, in some cases, even singly. The sew-holes on the limbs of the finest of them were set with brass grommets, to reinforce the points of stress.

Such dolls had to be treated with great care, and it is surprising, considering how easy it would be to damage them, that so many have survived to us in almost pristine condition. But then, surely, even amongst aristocratic children, these would have been their "best" dolls, to be looked at and admired, but not really played with!

This 7-inch wax lady doll, circa 1790, was made in the manner of late 18th century church figures. The body is a wire armature wrapped with linen strips and the head and limbs are poured wax. The eyes are drops of brown wax. *Coleman Collection.*

LEFT: A pair of commercially made German wax dolls, circa 1770, that have been used as ornaments in a decorative arbor made at home as a winter amusement. The man's eyes are painted and the lady's are glass beads. *Cora Ginsberg Collection.*

An English poured wax doll, circa1870. The hair, lashes and brows are set into the wax. *Collection of Margaret Whitton.*

LEFT: Two German poured wax dolls, circa1885-1890. They have mohair wigs and handmade clothes. Doll on the right: *Collection of the Museum of the City of New York.*

OPPOSITE PAGE: A German composition doll, circa 1875, with a lamb's-wool wig and wearing a commercially-made *robe de chambre*, a garment which could be worn at home without tight-laced corsets. *Collection of the Museum of the City of New York.*

A "Motschmann Baby"

This charming baby doll is one of those made in the mid-19th century in the manner patented by Motschmann of Sonneberg, in 1857, which was inspired in its turn by dolls of traditional Japanese design. Here, the wax is merely a finishing touch to a composition head, and most of the Mostschmann dolls are found without it.

The composition body has turned wooden limbs with articulated "floating" joints and the head contains a curious joint constructed with a series of interior tapes. A cloth mid-section in the torso allows a sqeaker to be accommodated. The design adheres closely to the Japanese original, even to the stylised, wavy wisps of hair over the ears.

His great charm is his costume, which is intact and pristine, and, we may note with interest, commercially made. Here, for once, we can hold in our hands the flimsy confectionery of net and glacé ribbon, still as delectable as it looks in paintings and fashion plates. This is the temporary prettiness, as fleeting as the freshness of cut flowers, of which we so often read: "To church in the heat, my old leghorn newly trimmed with rosebuds and a good blue feather..." and, "We spent the rest of the day mending our tarlatans, and planning their refurbishment."

The faded, sepia photographs of the period can look so dowdy, and the bright chromos are as unconvincing as the graceful, tidy little girls on valentines, as they clutch their crisp, beribboned dolls. But here is one of those dolls, still neat and pretty, and as absurd as one could wish. These elaborate, "best" toddlers' clothes were worn by girl and boy children alike, but the masculine nature of this toy implies that the child here is a little man. His pull-toy is also from Sonneberg, where these archaic-looking "baa-lambs" are still made to this day – although the rams of the species, like the one here with his beautiful gilt metal horns, seem now to be extinct. *Collection of the Museum of the City of New York.*

A German waxed "pumpkin head" of the 1860s is perfectly preserved inside a glass case. She sits on a mossy bank in a bower of cambric-leafed branches, accompanied by several colorful stuffed Carolina finches – a bird now extinct. This innocent group, once in my possession, was curiously dark and even sinister, a quality caught by the photograph. *Present owner unknown.*

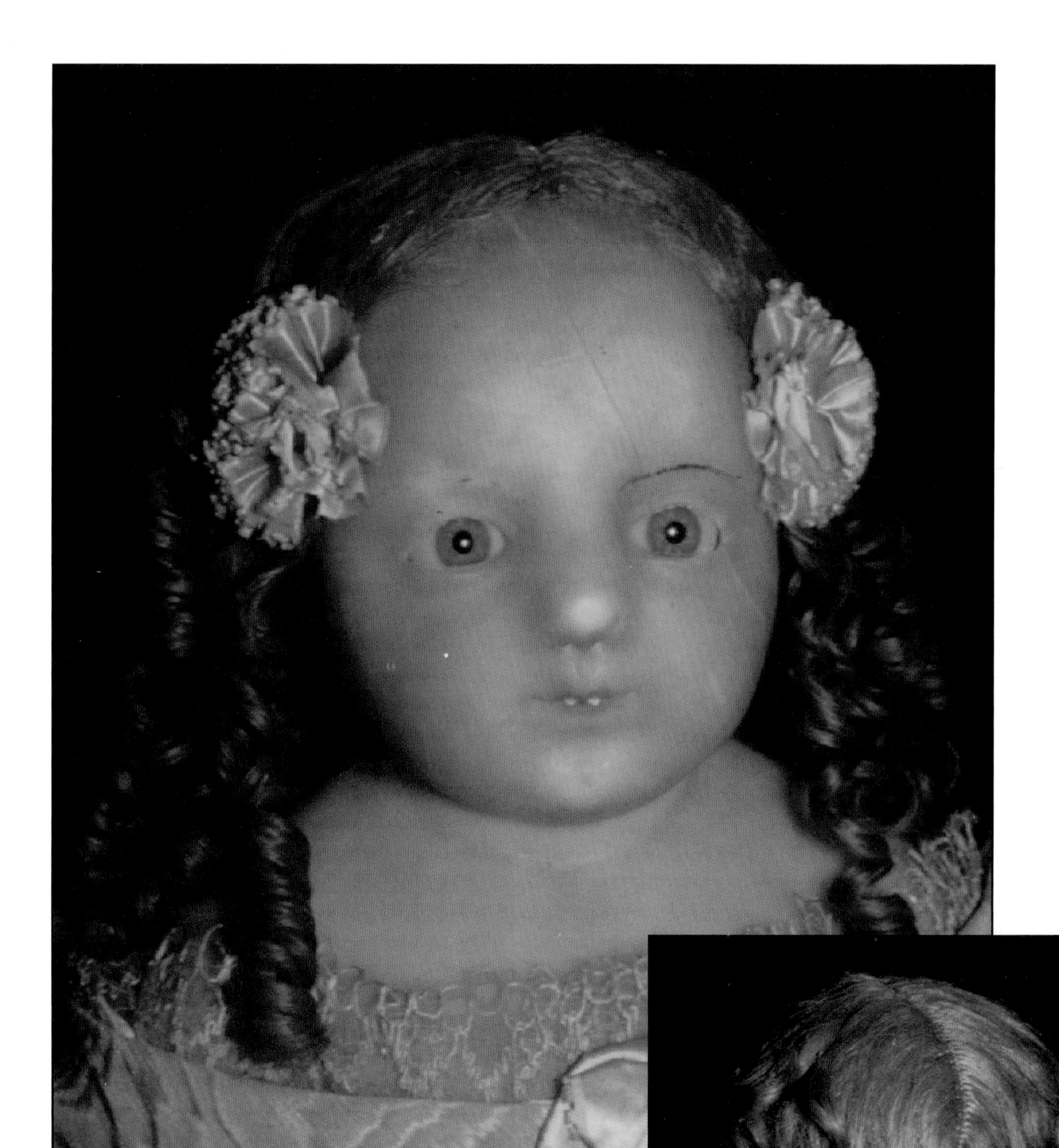

This ravishing English 28-inch poured wax doll has survived amazingly in perfect condition. The bloom is still on her cheeks, her wig has its sugar curls all in place, and her pretty dress is as fresh as the day when she first wore it. Her demure, dimpled smile reveals enchanting "buck" teeth. She has wired sleeping eyes. *Collection of Dorothy McGonagle.*

This beautiful wax dates from the mid-19th century, and is almost certainly of German origin. She is untouched and perfect, but the most astonishing detail is her elaborate mohair wig, which by some miracle is as fresh and neat as when it was first arranged, all those years ago. *Collection of Michael Canadas.*

Epilogue

Fresh as Springtime

Doll making in France is an industry that seems to have become grown-up and important very quickly during the 1850s. There were, of course, French dolls made before this date, but not on any grand scale.

The sudden rise of this major industry was directly related to the efforts of the Empress Eugenie to encourage the luxury trades of her country. It is well known that she deliberately launched some of the most extravagant styles of the mid-century, including the ever-swelling crinolines, exotic fabrics, and new, expensive colours. This she did, not for personal aggrandisement as her predecessors had done, but in an attempt to re-establish the French silk industry and to create a world market for its products. As a result, even today, a French label implies luxury and refinement. And from the first, the French lady dolls were the epitome of this elegance.

These dolls did indeed represent the most elegant ladies imaginable. They seem to have sprung into existence overnight and with apparently no background. It is known that the china heads and limbs of some of the pioneers were in fact commissioned and imported from German manufacturers, although this state of affairs did not last for long. But suddenly, there were dolls in the shops which were unlike any that had existed before, their structure a synthesis of the skills employed in many of the decorative arts for which France was famous. The potter, the joiner, the wigmaker, the tailor, and especially the dressmaker were all important contributing craftsmen to these beautiful lady dolls.

It is hard to credit that such elaborate perfection should have sprung forth, like Athene from her father's head, full grown. One feels that surely there must have been hesitant, experimental stages in which the dolls were simple, perhaps even crude. But if so, there were so few of them that they quickly disappeared, or else they were so dissimilar that they survive unrecognised.

Most of the earliest examples, the exquisite Hurets and Rhomers, for instance, have glazed china heads with painted eyes. They are poised and cool, and they seem well aware of their excellence – indeed, of their superiority. They displayed from the outset a variety of materials, and the ingenuity of their construction suggests eager, imaginative experiment. Once started, the luxury doll makers seem to have worked in a frenzy of enthusiasm as one exquisite model after another left their hands. Their dolls became increasingly lavish in concept and unstinting in their consumption of labour. They were always expensive – sometimes fantastically so – and they were aimed both at the aristocracy and at the newly prosperous middle classes everywhere.

The repressive figure of Queen Victoria, together with the impoverished state of Europe in the aftermath of the Napoleonic Wars, has given a misleadingly repressive aura to at least one half of the 19th century. But by 1850, the general picture was by no means demure and the new zest for display and conspicuous consumption affected everyone. The aristocracy still lived in unfettered ease in every country, and the middle classes aped them to the fullest extent of their pockets.

Below the subtle yet decisive line that removed the gentry from the rest, no one was so poor that he or she could not make some attempt to "cut a dash." In the poorer quarters of London to this day, this impulse if still very strong. The meanest streets display fine curtains and fresh flowers in brightly polished windows, belying the poverty and perhaps hardship in the room behind. And it is a poor-spirited factory girl who cannot appear on Sunday dressed to kill!

This mania for display accelerated through the 1870s and 1880s, embracing the spectrum of the family, including the children. For every little girl of this time, be she rich or not so rich, the possession of a fine French doll represented the height of luxury.

It can be claimed that the 1850s ushered in a new era, both in England and on the Continent. There was a springtime freshness in the air, a new optimism.

The Dolls of Maison Huret

These two enchanting dolls are both unmarked, but they are of a type associated with Maison Huret, known to have been making dolls in Paris since 1850. This possible origin for these two beauties is strengthened, in the case of the larger doll, by the fact that she possesses an elegant trunk with the elaborate paper label of Maison Huret. It is full of clothes and accessories, and the dresses, which fit the doll perfectly, all have the Huret label with the markings stamped in gilt.

Both dolls have stitched, white kid bodies with glazed china heads, shoulderplates and forearms. The modelling is exquisite, the painting light and deft. The brilliance of the under-glaze colours is enhanced by the inset glass eyes with their rich, blue irises. These heads have a curiously insouciant air, reminiscent of the frivolous porcelain "toys" of the previous century.

The clothing is original to both dolls, and in both cases is remarkably fine. One wonders if the beautiful pink silk is from Lyons; the skirt here is mounted on a heavier lining, so that the effect is bouffant. The ribbons and frills are light-hearted, but not fussy. The grey dress is fine, smooth wool with a silken weft, and features a closely-woven stripe. If this fabric could be identified, it would be found to have one of those charming and characteristic names like "bombazine." "jaconet," or "grenadine." The pink shawl is a woollen web so fine that it will drift in the air. The identical straw hats are trimmed in the fashionable manner with ribbons, and with rosettes beneath their brims.

Both dolls are from the Toy Collection of the Museum of the City of New York.

The Rohmer Dolls

Mlle. Marie Antoinette Leontine Rohmer is known to have been making dolls at least as early as 1857, when she was granted a patent for elaborate dolls' bodies, but she must have begun her career some years earlier.

The doll here in the blue dress has the mark of Rohmer stamped across her bosom. She has a wooden body covered smoothly with white kid and precisely jointed. Her head, shoulderplate, forearms and lower legs are all made of glazed china. The neck has the flat, so-called cup-and-saucer joint that is often found on the Rohmer dolls. The face is alert and distinctive, its modelling very subtle, as is that of the exquisite hands and feet.

None of the clothing is original. The striped cotton dress, which is labelled "Huret, Paris," belongs to the larger Huret doll in the first picture here, as do the hat and accessories. The blue-checked silk dress is original to the period but was not made for this doll – in fact, is slightly too large for her.

Both dolls are from the Toy Collection of the Museum of the City of New York.

I love a paradox, and here in my Epilogue is an amusing paradox. To misquote T. S. Eliot, "In my end is a new beginning."

As was hinted in the last chapter, I chose the era for my closure very carefully, the moment in the long and enchanting history of doll making that seems to me to be a watershed, reflecting faithfully a profound change in the lifestyles, first of Europe, and then of America and indeed, eventually of the entire civilized world.

Those Napoleonic Wars, which seem so remote and primitive, even romantic to me from this distance, were in fact devastating both politically and economically, and together with the inexorable advance of the industrial revolution, had created a violent disruption of the ancient aristocratic system, a disruption the effect of which was to be long lasting, indeed, still to be felt right up to this very day.

Europe slowly recovered from the devastation, and prosperity began to dawn after the "hungry" 1840s. National pride began to reassert itself, but it was clear that there was now a new class emerging, that of the high-powered industrialist. By the 1850s this new class was entrenched, and there was new money in the shape of great fortunes all over Europe, and before many decades on an even larger scale, in America.

This shifting of power became very clear with the opening of the Great Exhibition in the astonishing Crystal Palace in London, England, in 1851. Here, for all the world to see was the first demonstration of the principle of "Conspicuous Display," which was to have such a profound effect on decorative arts everywhere, a principle which was only outmoded by the equally disruptive effects on society produced by World War I.

Amidst all the lavishness of furniture at the exhibition, of costly glass and china, of fabrics and fountains, of water closets and railway coaches, could be seen the first of the "Conspicuous Display" dolls. Before this time, the only costly dolls had been made for princesses and young aristocrats. But here, at the Great Exhibition, were the first of the luxury dolls that were to set the standards, and indeed, to become the inspiration for doll makers for the rest of the century.

There was instituted at this time a sharp distinction between dolls to be played with and dolls that were status symbols. I suspect that the reason why so many of the fine French lady dolls and the later German equivalents exist today in superb condition, is that they were in fact nursery "real estate," dolls bought to demonstrate the wealth and power of the child's parents. Some of those children, who grew up during "la Belle Époque," that golden period of the reign of Edward the Seventh in England, can still remember those status dolls.

Barbara Cartland, for instance, has nostalgic memories of her own splendid dolls. "They were kept locked away," she reminisces, "but when my mother had teatime visitors, I was dressed in my best finery and led by my nurse to the drawing room door. There, a wonderful French doll was put in my arms, and I sat on a chair and held it gingerly while the visitors talked to me. I stayed ten or fifteen minutes, and then was escorted out again by my nurse – and the doll was instantly taken away. I know it was beautiful, but I barely saw it!"

So, in my end is a new beginning. The freshness of springtime represented here flowered and ripened into a parade of the most spectacular dolls that were ever made. And those superb dolls from the second half of the 19th century – that golden age—could and I hope will provide a rich source for a companion volume to this one, with rare and lovely dolls in abundance!

So I hope, and it is with this alluring prospect that I take my leave,

John Darcy Noble

The manufacturer of this lovely glazed china doll is still uncertain, but it has characteristics that point to Jacob Petit, French maker of costly porcelain figurines. Besides this child, there is also the lady doll on page 106. Both are from the early 1850s, and both are very rare. *Author's collection.*

About the Author

John Darcy Noble

John Darcy Noble was born in 1923 in Greenwich, a suburb of London on the river Thames, which at that time was still a Dickensian backwater. This creative little boy grew up well aware of and fascinated by the tangible relics of gas-lit London. Even his bedtime was signaled by the arrival of the street lamplighter, immortalized by Robert Louis Stevenson in the poem that John Darcy knew by heart.

He began to collect old toys when he was six years old, trading a nice new puzzle with a schoolmate, who had a curious china whistle, dating from about 1860, in the shape of a cigar with a little naked "Frozen Charlie" doll sitting astride it. That treasured whistle, still in John Darcy's possession, was soon joined by many other old toys. By the time he was ten, he could be said to have a toy collection, and by the time he was 16, it was a very nice collection indeed. In the meantime he had discovered how to research and had taught himself much about those old playthings that he loved.

John Darcy graduated from London University with a Master's degree in Fine Art, and by the mid-1950s was teaching in London's art schools, and had held several one-man shows of his haunting, decorative paintings in London and Paris. In the latter part of the decade he helped to mount exhibitions of old toys for the Royal Society for the Blind. Since this august institution was sponsored by several royal duchesses he was accorded much publicity for doing so, and received even more, when, with very little capital or backing, he helped Margerite Fawdrey to create Pollock's Toy Museum, the first of its kind in England.

He came to the United States in 1960 and has never gone back—not surprisingly, since within a few months of his arrival he was offered the position of Curator of the Toy Collection at the Museum of the City of New York, a position he was to hold for nearly 30 years. During this time his charismatic exhibitions, together with the drawing power of his writings and lectures on the subject so dear to his heart, have made that Toy Collection famous throughout the world.

Now retired and living happily in a quiet, countrified part of Southern California, John Darcy continues to take a passionate interest in old dolls and toys. He spends sunny days as he has always done, painting and writing, and delighting in his own rarified collection of these fascinating relics of past childhood. He has always loved and made paper dolls and his published examples in this field are avidly collected.

Index